The Hargrove Family History

by Tara Hargrove

An exhibit at the Nelson-Atkins Museum of Art
December 2012 - March 2013

Edited by Bryan Colley.

Photos by Bryan Colley unless otherwise noted.

Expanded Edition Copyright © 2013 by Tara Varney and Bryan Colley.

ISBN: 978-1-300-57982-3

Published by KC Stage, PO Box 410492, Kansas City, Missouri 64141-0492, www.kcstage.com

www.jupiterkansas.com

Contents

Introduction

Every family has a story. These stories can contain elements that are fascinating, inspiring, and humorous. Other elements can be confusing, embarrassing, and illegal. Many times, we are tempted to highlight some elements, and conveniently forget to mention the others.

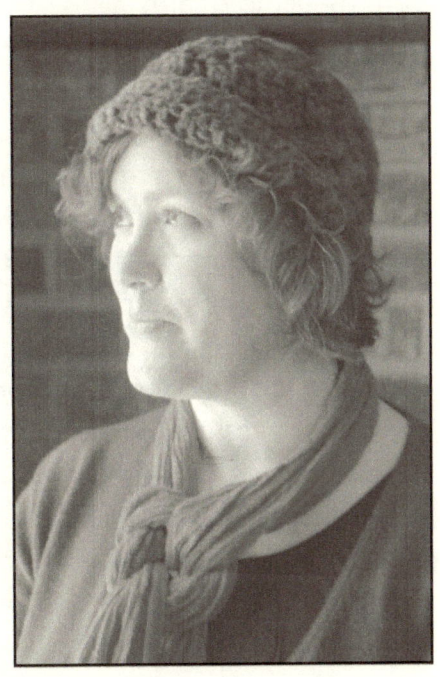

One of the elements that binds the Hargroves together is their love of collecting beautiful and interesting items. Since my great-great-great-great grandfather, Perry Hargrove, came to this country at age six, every generation of the Hargrove family has had a member that represented an interest in art: collecting, importing, dealing, creating, authenticating, preserving, and even forging it. At every turn, the Hargroves exemplified their time in the evolution of the American museum, from personal collection, to Cabinets of Curiosities, to securing items for the permanent collections of major museums, to advocating for the rights of Native peoples to retain ownership of their cultural heritage.

Setting out to record my family's history wasn't a journey that I was 100% sure I wanted to go on. I knew there were scoundrels in our past, even a convict and a murderer. I wanted to discover the truth about myself and my heritage, and I wanted to be able to speak it plainly, but I didn't want to step on anyone's toes. I'm a storyteller by trade; would I be able to separate fact from fiction, and personal prejudices from the simple tale?

What I discovered is that, by and large, people are just people. They do the best they can. The scoundrel was in love with fantasy. The convict couldn't handle his feelings of worthlessness, and the murderer... well, the murderer shot his brother in cold blood. I can't defend that. Still, it's part of the truth, part of my family's history, and so, it's part of me.

Sometimes, the stories of my family are dark and troubling. Sometimes, they are entertaining and illuminating. They are all Hargrove though, and together, they wend their way toward creating a passionate history of believing in the power of art to transform lives, and the world.

My biggest thanks and deepest love for my multi-talented brother, Bryan, for all his help on this book. Thanks, also, for handing me tissues when I cried, and a beer when I laughed. You're the best, bro.

Tara Hargrove

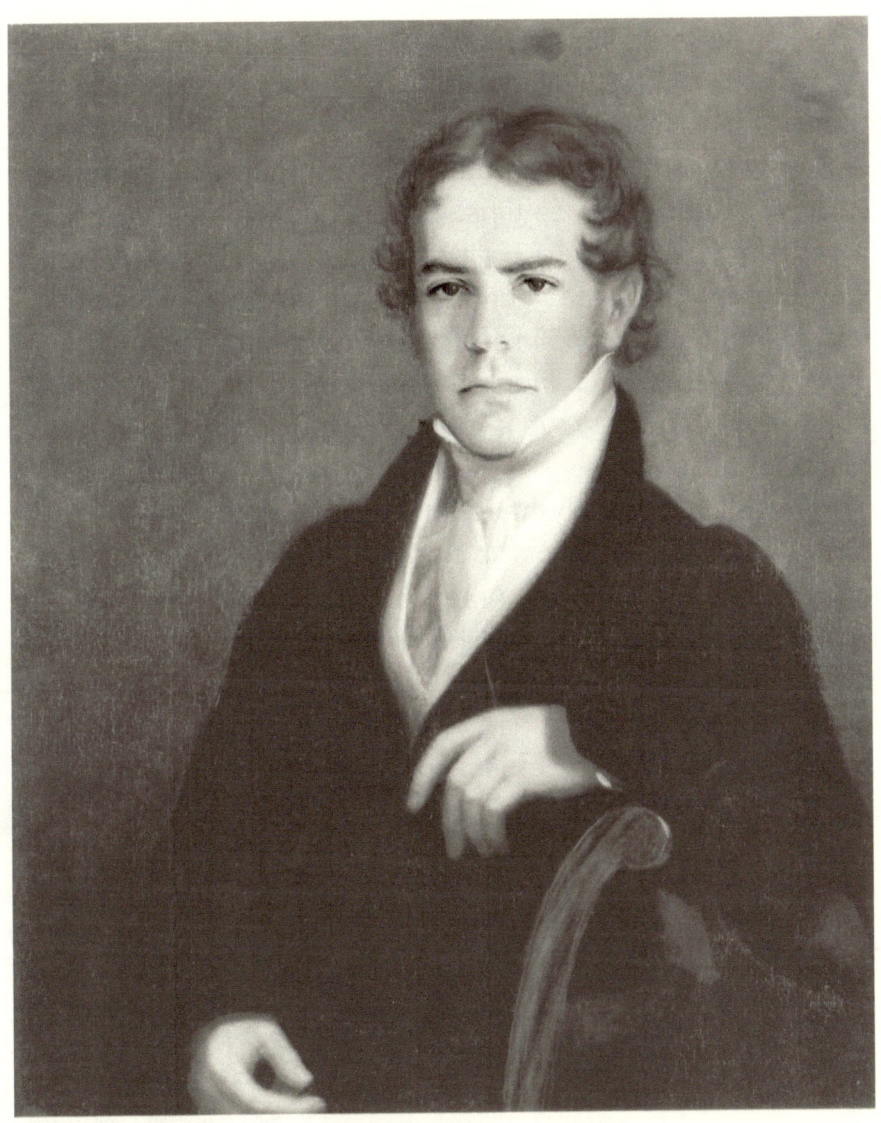

Perry Hargrove (1776-1825)

1809 painting by Charles Bird King, on display at the University of Pennsylvania.

Perry Hargrove was heir to the Hargrove Textiles fortune and, in 1782, sailed with his family from England to the United States, where they established themselves in Philadelphia. His father, Nathan Hargrove, dabbled in politics during his free time. The Hargrove home became a gathering place for the political elite, and young Perry was well-known among the country's forefathers, as he would entertain by playing violin and telling outrageous and opinionated stories. Benjamin Franklin once remarked, "A conversation with young Hargrove is more enlightening than with any member of Congress."

Perry fell in love with the rough new country. Taking his birthdate of July 4, 1776 as a sign, he began collecting objects and trinkets related to the American Revolution, which he would boast about with his schoolmates and visitors. He could display any object and tell exactly how he acquired it, who gave it to him, and what particularly important event happened on that day. The objects became a diary of his youth.

Nathan Hargrove (1740-1801)

Moved to the United States in 1782 to establish a textile trade with England.

Henrietta Hanson (1750-1812)

The Hanson family was well-regarded in Surrey, where they produced cheese.

Charles Hargrove (1768-1846)

Ran for the Pennsylvania Senate but lost the race to William Findlay.

Edward Hargrove (1770-1825)

Maintained the family textile business in Philadelphia.

Perry Hargrove (1776-1825)

Early authority on the American Revolution. He taught history at the University of Pennsylvania.

When his father constructed a new stable on their estate, he let Perry move his growing collection into the old out-building. Perry began collecting in earnest, amassing one of the largest and most comprehensive histories of early America at that time. By the mid-1790s, it was customary for wealthy visitors to Philadelphia to pay a visit to Perry's stable, and hear him tell tales of his youthful encounters with presidents, senators, and other influential persons, accompanied by such rarities as George Washington's wig, John Adams' spade, or his prized possession, the quill pen used by Thomas Jefferson to write the Declaration of Independence.

As the textile trade grew, Perry was charged with handling more and more of his father's operations. It was a task he cared little about, and he didn't appreciate taking time away from his collecting. At 27, he married Anne Witherspoon, the daughter of a Connecticut lawyer. They had four children: Josiah,

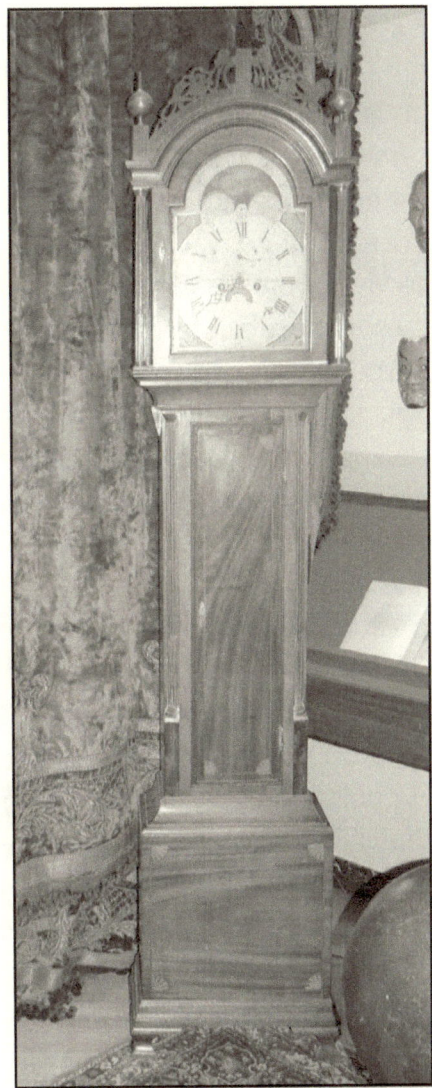

Simon Willard , American, 1800-1810, Mahogany

Perry's father, was good friends with John and Abigail Adams. John was often in the group entertained by young Perry. Perry's first child, Josiah, was born in 1809, and the Adams' gifted Nathan's widow, Anne, with a Simon Willard clock to commemorate the occasion. When she passed away in 1812, the clock came into Perry's possession.

Evangeline, Edgar, and Thaddeus, but Anne spent as much time looking after her husband's collection as she did the household.

In his 20s, Hargrove became a walking encyclopedia of early America's history, especially the Revolution. Many were surprised that he was too young to have lived through the war, so vivid were his descriptions of the events, always backed up by some artifact from the battlefield. During the War of 1812, Perry eagerly abandoned his family business and took up arms against the British on the Canadian frontier. Along the way, he scavenged artifacts and treasures that he sent back home to his wife. He even witnessed the 1814 burning of Washington, and saved some of the burnt timbers of the White House for his collection.

After the war, Perry took a position teaching history at the University of Pennsylvania, using his objects to relate the events of the revolution. By this time, his collection had grown so large that it completely filled the old stable on his estate. He planned to use his inheritance to construct a building on the University campus to house the collection, and make it accessible to students and the public alike. Unfortunately, during a fireworks celebration on July 4, 1818, the old stable caught fire and Perry's entire collection was destroyed.

Without the artifacts, Perry found he could no longer remember historical events and had to resign from the University: "My memories reside within the artifacts, and without them my mind is empty. It is as if I had never lived." Despondent, Perry admitted himself into an asylum, and died in 1825 at the age of 49.

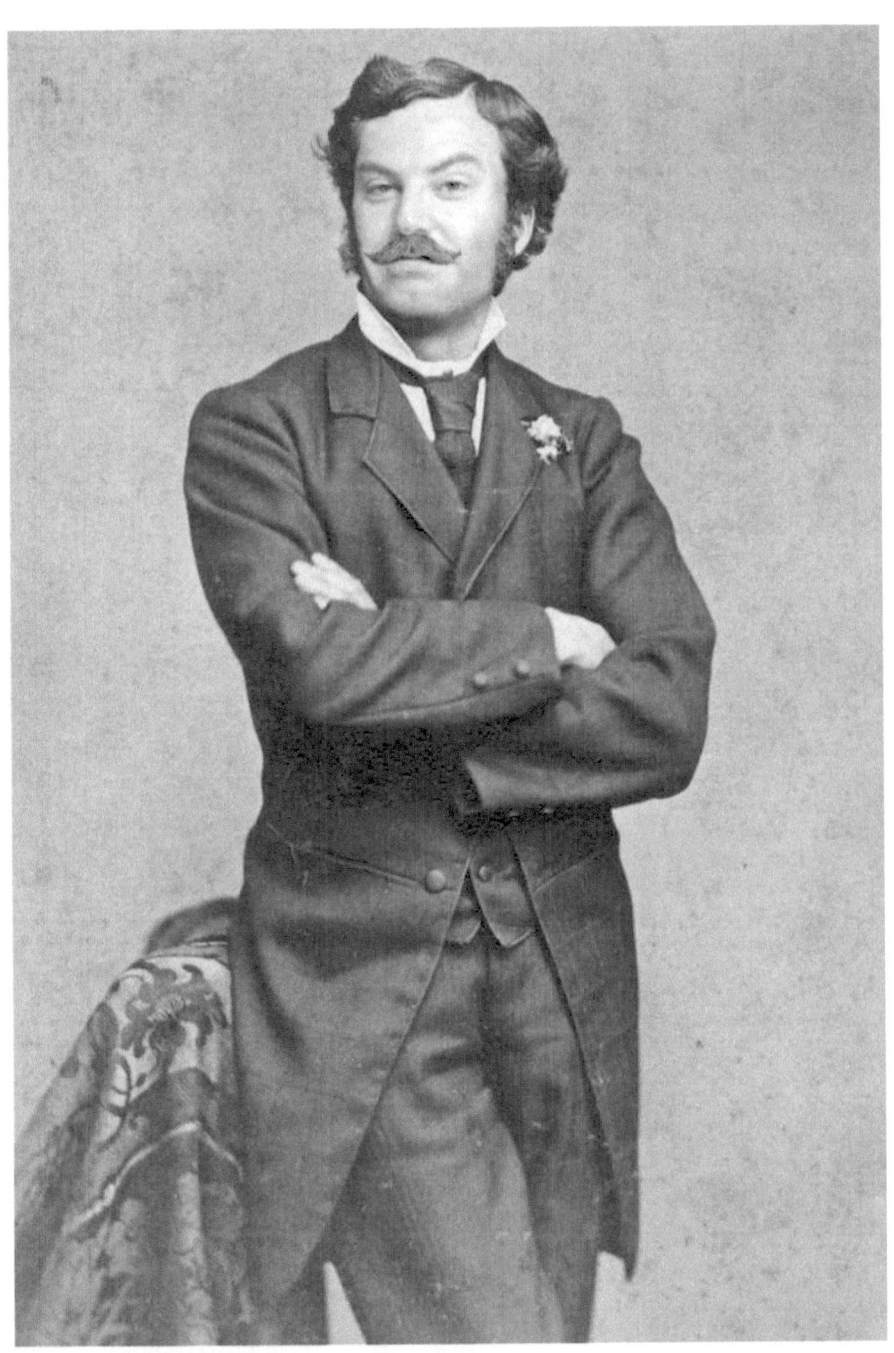

Edgar Hargrove (1809-1854)

Restored studio potrait of Edgar Hargrove taken in 1848.

E dgar was the third of four children, and he was the only one that possessed the famous collecting habit of his father, but Edgar's tastes were decidedly more controversial. When given an object of a particular novelty, he would make up fantastic tales, offering just enough truth to make the story believable. The tales would often involve murder and intrigue, evil curses, daring heists, and adventures in far-away lands. In this way he could take an ordinary trinket and sell it for many times its value, or even better, use it to seduce an enticing young lady.

He also developed a taste for finely crafted and rare artifacts, and some said he was as gullible as he was conniving. He would spend enormous amounts on religious relics, fine works of art, and other odd treasures. He squandered his family fortunes until his elder brother, Josiah, who had inherited

Perry Hargrove (1776-1825)

Anne Witherspoon (1785-1833)

The daughter of a Connecticut lawyer, Anne organized social events for Perry.

Josiah Hargrove (1804-1871)

Maintained the family textile business until it went bankrupt after the Civil War.

Evangeline Hargrove (1806-1860)

Married a wealthy Philadelphia banker who was an early investor in railroads.

Edgar Hargrove (1809-1854)

Collector of art and oddities who traveled the Atlantic seaboard performing feats of magic and seducing women.

Thaddeus Hargrove (1810-1813)

Died of smallpox during the War of 1812 while Perry was away in Canada.

the family business, cut him off from all income, causing a rift that kept Edgar away from the family for many years. Left to fend for himself, he took his priceless artifacts and began traveling throughout the states, displaying his "Cabinet of Curiosities" to paying onlookers and entertaining high society with stories from the cabinet and impressive feats of magic.

He gained a reputation as a seducer of women, a shyster, and, in one formal complaint to the city leaders of Saratoga Springs, "an agent of the devil" – all of which only increased his mystique and popularity in the public eye. His taste for finer things made him an amateur dealer in art and artifacts and he maintained several wealthy clients in his travels.

In 1838, he met a dark-haired beauty, Elma, while traveling through Georgia. They eventually married and moved to Baltimore, where Edgar maintained

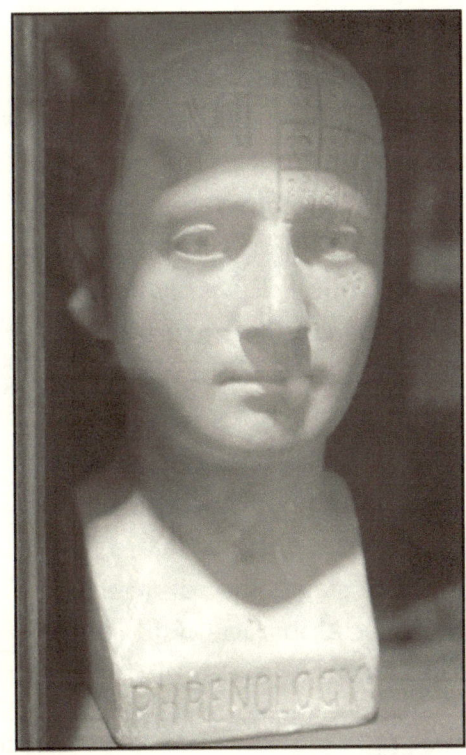

Phrenology was a pseudo-science, popular in the early- to mid-1800s, that focused on the measurements of the human skull, and how they described brain functions, intelligence, personality, and various psychological tendencies such as religion and vocation.

Featured in Edgar Hargrove's traveling "Cabinet of Curiosities," this phrenology bust was highlighted in the "Moderne Sciences" section. For a fee, Edgar examined the skulls of patrons and, after they paid an additional amount, he provided them with the report of his findings. Edgar variously claimed to have developed the study of phrenology himself, been a co-founder of the field, and to have been the mentored Franz Joseph Gall, who actually developed the field of phrenology in Europe before Edgar was born.

a modest home filled with art and treasures. Due to his extravagant tastes, his connections admitted them into high society. Elma, a recluse who spent many months alone while Edgar traveled, was regarded as mysterious and exotic – a reputation enhanced by her shyness.

After Edgar's extensive travels in the south, where he witnessed the cruel treatment of slaves, he returned to Philadelphia to confront his long-estranged older brother, Josiah. He claimed that the Hargrove family business, which milled cotton picked by slaves and shipped textiles to England and several other countries, was a "violation of human decency" and urged his brother to join the abolitionist movement. During a heated debate, Edgar was shot. Claiming self-defense and playing on Edgar's sordid reputation, Josiah was not prosecuted. He remained pro-slavery throughout the Civil War, but Hargrove Textiles went bankrupt when the conflict was over.

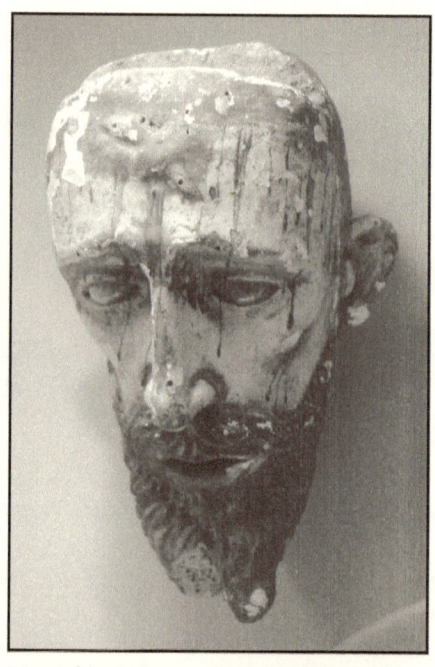

Most likely brought to the United States by a returning missionary, this Spanish colonial head of Jesus came into Edgar's possession in the 1840s. It was once attached to the rest of the figure, but was apparently separated by the time Edgar became the owner. He often told the story of "tears" that appeared in the eyes of the head that coordinated with times of personal weakness. Edgar claimed that the head was given to him by a grateful nun after he donated a large sum of money to an orphanage, but it's more likely that he actually bought the head from a thief. Although stealing was not usually his M.O., it cannot be ruled out that Edgar himself was the thief in question.

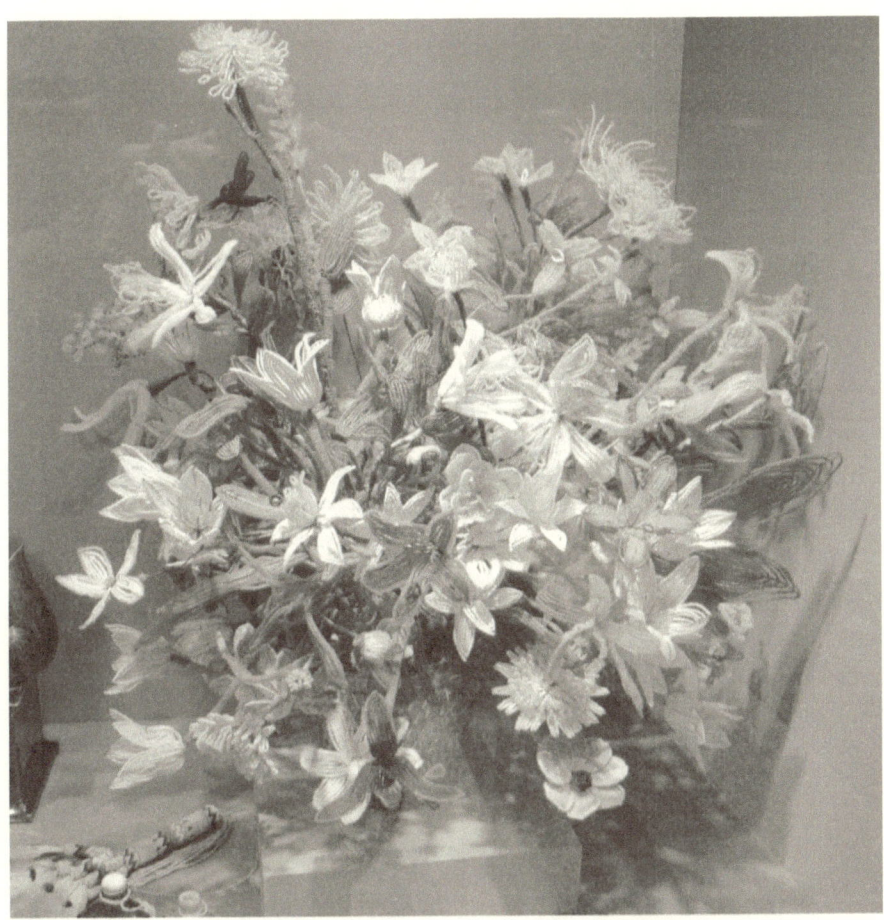

These beaded flowers were made by Elma, Edgar's wife. She stayed at home while he traveled the South with his Cabinet of Curiosities. She had a lot of time on her hands. A lot!

Following Edgar's death, Elma discovered that her husband was deeply in debt, and was forced to sell most of his artifacts to maintain their lifestyle and raise their son, Mortimer. Some of the works of art that Edgar had once possessed are now worth millions.

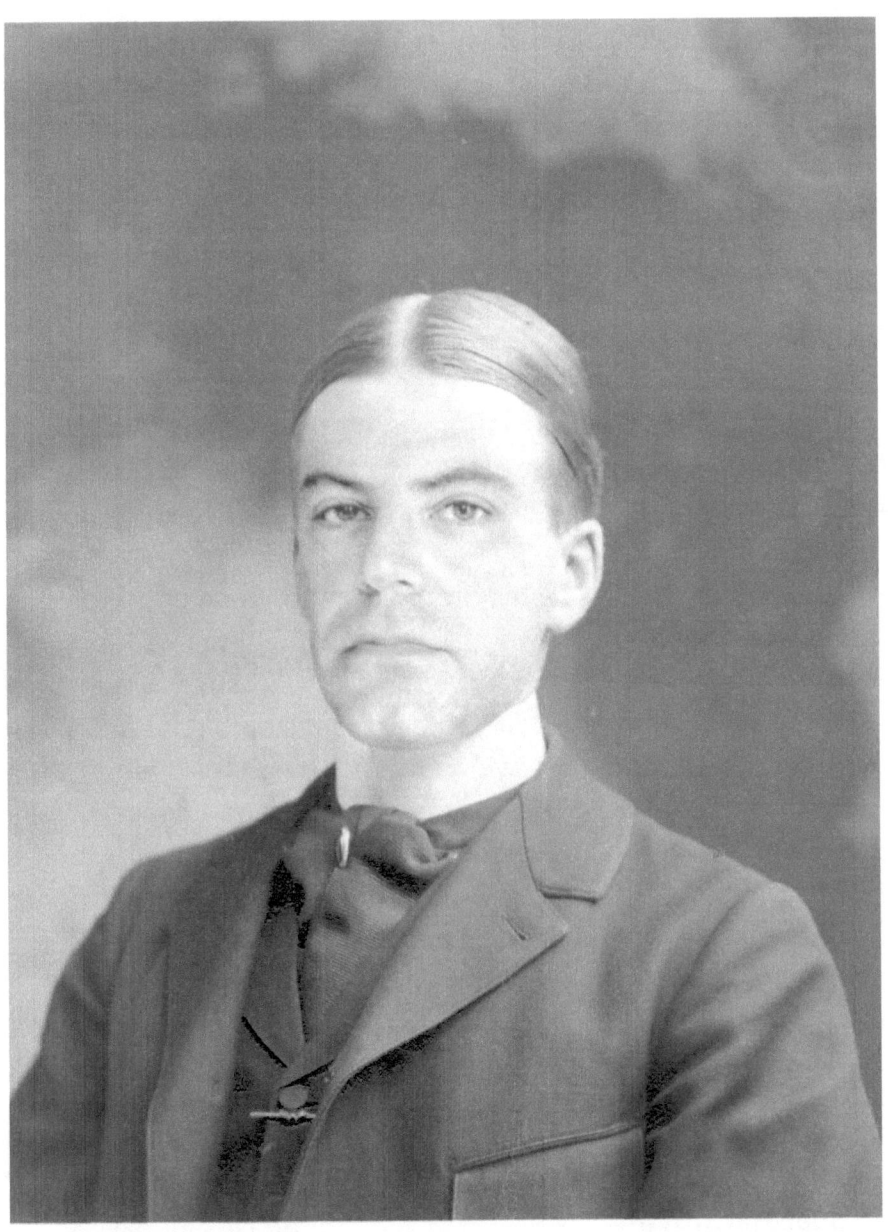

Mortimer Hargrove (1840-1898)

Portrait of Mortimer Hargrove taken in the 1880s.

The only child of Edgar and Elma Hargrove, Mortimer Hessell Hargrove grew up surrounded with art and artifacts that his parents could scarcely afford. Edgar traveled extensively as an art dealer, and when he returned, he filled the house with fanciful tales of his journeys, the elite with whom he spent his time, and detailed descriptions of the "lives" of the artifacts that he brought back with him. Mortimer accompanied his father on a few trips, but found the lifestyle unpleasantly erratic, so he preferred to stay home with his somewhat withdrawn mother. Introverted himself, Mortimer spent most of his time alone, reading history books, and writing stories of imagined private lives of historical figures.

After Edgar's death by his brother's hand, Elma and Mortimer, aged fourteen, moved to New York City to live with cousins. To make ends meet, Mortimer found employment at the local mercantile, cleaning up after closing time every night, and Elma took in sewing and mending jobs. Due to the debt that Edgar had incurred with his extravagant lifestyle, Elma was also forced to sell much of her husband's collection of art. Since she was unschooled in the ways of art dealing, her ignorance was often exploited and she was not paid the full value of the works.

Mortimer fell in love with Geneva Beatrice Johnston, a quiet and intelligent local seamstress. It is believed that Geneva was the only person with whom Mortimer ever shared his stories.

Edgar Hargrove (1809-1854)

Elma Hessell (1810-1873)

Dark Southern beauty drawn to
Edgar's mysterious lifestyle.

Mortimer Hargrove (1840-1898)

Janitor at the Metropolitan Museum
of Art in New York City.

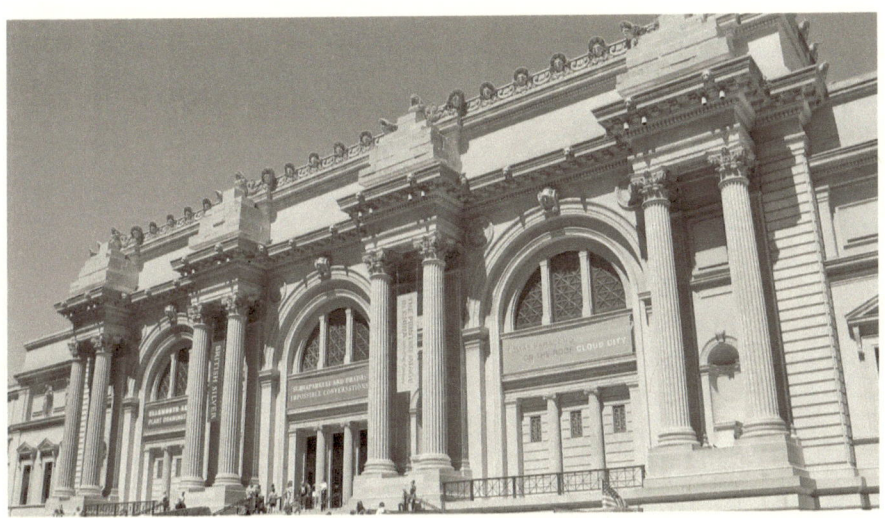

The Metropolitan Museum of Art in New York City opened in 1872.

The two were married in 1862, and suffered a series of emotional and financial setbacks early in their marriage. Geneva endured two miscarriages and doctors were unsure of her body's ability to carry a child to term. In 1864, a daughter, Ola Mae, was born prematurely, and died moments later. A healthy son, Gideon, was born in 1866, but he contracted smallpox and died when he was two years old. In grief, Mortimer plunged himself into his writing again.

On January 18, 1870, Geneva delivered a healthy baby boy, whom they named Gilbert. In 1872, Mortimer found employment as a janitor at the newly-opened Metropolitan Museum of Art. They moved into their own apartment, and later that year, Geneva gave birth to Wilhelmina. Daughter Theodora joined the family in 1874.

Mortimer worked at the museum until his death from accidental asphyxiation of solvent fumes in 1898. By then, all the children were grown and out of the house, and Geneva took in the laundry of some of the well-to-do in the area to make ends meet. In 1914, Geneva passed away in her sleep at the age of 73.

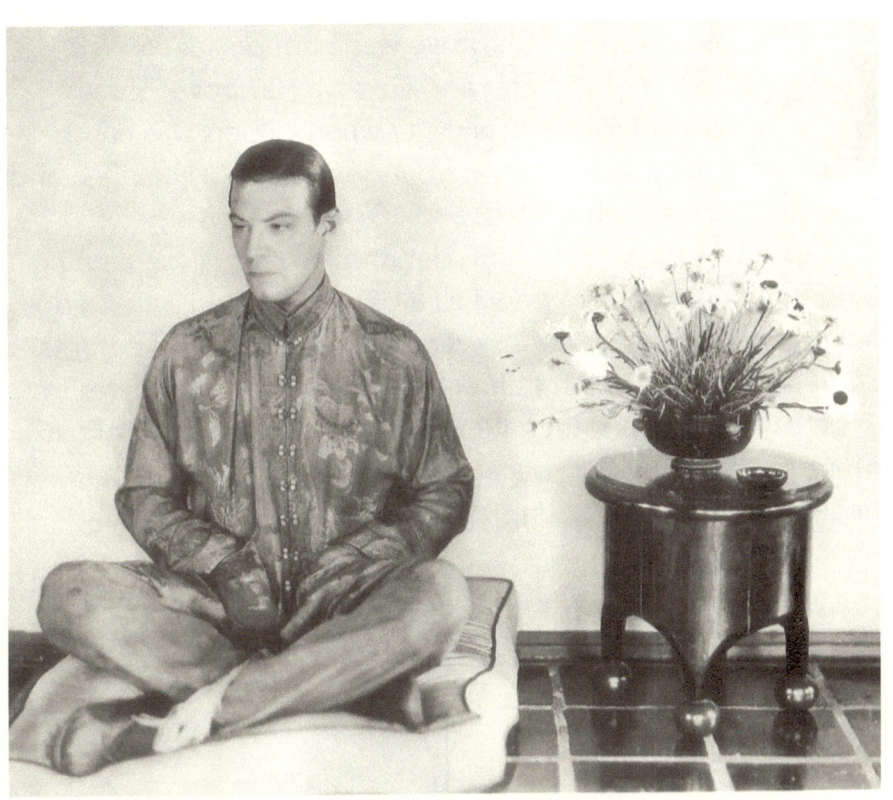

Gilbert Hargrove (1870-1940)

Photo of Gilbert Hargrove in Shanghai taken sometime between 1908 and 1912

G ilbert Gabriel Hargrove was born on January 18, 1870 to Mortimer and Geneva Hargrove. They moved to New York City when Gilbert was an infant. Gilbert's two younger sisters, Wilhelmina and Theodora, were born in 1872 and 1874, respectively.

Gilbert was a good student, but mischievous, soon earning a reputation among his peers as a boy who would dare to do anything for a penny. After several broken bones, his parents started keeping a much tighter leash on their young daredevil.

Often visiting his father at his workplace, the Metropolitan Museum of Art, Gilbert became entranced by objects from faraway places, later noting, "Each object seemed to quiver,

Mortimer Hargrove (1840-1898)

Geneva Johnston (1841-1914)

Worked as a seamstress
in New York City.

Ola Mae Hargrove (1864)

Died during childbirth.

Gideon Hargrove (1866-1868)

Died at the age of two from smallpox.

Gilbert Hargrove (1870-1940)

Famed world explorer and art collector who traveled the Old West and China. Inspired the character of Indiana Jones.

Wilhelmina Hargrove (1872-1890)

Eloped with an iron worker at the age of 15 and moved to Johnstown, Pennsylvania, where she died in the Johnstown flood.

Theodora Hargrove (1874-1932)

Worked as a milliner for Caroline Reboux and joined the women's suffrage movement.

begging to tell the stories of their lives." As he grew older, his adventurous nature turned to restlessness, and he longed to explore the world.

At the age of sixteen, Gilbert left home. By early 1888 he had made his way to Kansas City and found a job writing obituaries at the *Kansas City Times*. He had an amazing eye for detail, and was often commended for accuracy, so it wasn't long before he was promoted to beat reporter.

Working at a newspaper exposed him to stories of events, places, and people that fueled his desire to travel. When the story broke, in December of 1890, that Sitting Bull had been killed during an arrest, Gilbert was able to convince his editor to let him be the one to cover the story.

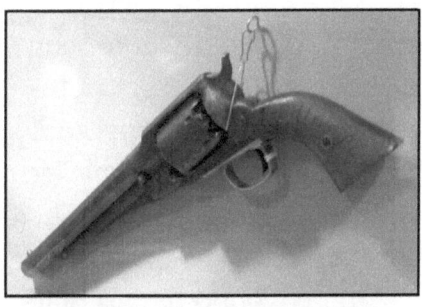

In late 1890, Gilbert traveled northwest to cover the death of Sitting Bull. At first, he was dismissive of the Native Americans' less comfortable life, but quickly warmed, and his newspaper articles in defense of Native Americans became quite impassioned. Sioux leaders realized they had an ally. As thanks, he was awarded a gun that once belonged to Sitting Bull himself. It immediately became his most prized treasure. Gilbert considered it a lucky charm, and never traveled without it.

Early in the cold, difficult journey northwest, Gilbert wrote that "…looking out over this vast, hard, empty land, I covet a warm, soft bed more desperately than any coin or tale." Over the next few months, however, as he began to immerse himself in the culture and speak to witnesses of Sitting Bull's death and the Wounded Knee Massacre, he began to sympathize with the plight of the native peoples. This changed

Years later, after he became a father, he shared with his young twin sons the magnificent piece of history. When it was returned to him later that evening, he found that "Sitting Bull" had been carved crudely into the stock. He was furious at the vandalism, but the boys joined forces and refused to divulge the culprit.

attitude was reflected in the series of columns he sent back to the newspaper about his journey. In March of 1891, he wrote of the Lakota, "As for the people, they are of extraordinary strength, beauty, and wisdom. Savages they most definitely are not. Unlike the European encroachers, they take nothing in this world for granted. Everyday objects are imbued with spirit and character. Their lives are art."

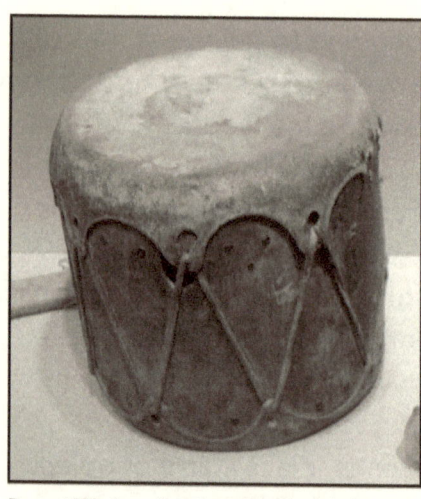

Drum, 1875; Santo Domingo; Wood, rawhide, native leather, brass tacks, iron nails, and pigment

This Pueblo drum has been passed down from one generation of Hargrove to another ever since Gilbert brought it to San Francisco with him after wandering the west. The sides of the drums are painted with the faces of cloud gods.

After covering Sitting Bull's death, Gilbert gave up his job with the *Kansas City Times* and made his home out west, working briefly for the *Rocky Mountain News* before getting caught up in the gold rush at Cripple Creek. He lived a rugged life panning for gold and then mining silver, until silver prices went bust in 1893.

Eager to seek new adventures, Gilbert wandered the west. Quarter and company was easy to find, as Hargrove befriended Native Americans of various tribes with his knack for languages and admiration of culture. There is little historical information about Gilbert's years out west, except his own exaggerated accounts of staring down danger on a daily basis. Gilbert's West was full of deadly rattlesnakes, attacking bears, life-threatening snowstorms, skirmishes with warring Indians, run-ins with bandits, and far too many other harrowing adventures to be believed. However, he did provide a good account of Native American customs, and spoke at least five different tribal languages.

As he learned more about the conditions under which the American government was forcing native people to live, Hargrove became enamored of Native Americans and their culture, and grew more concerned about their fate. His deepening attachment resulted in collecting objects created by various Native American nations. As when he was a child, and felt connected to the objects in the museum, Hargrove found a bond with the people to whom objects belonged. He began trading whatever he had on hand—candy, jewelry, photos, paper and pens—for Native American creations.

In 1897, at the age of 27, Hargrove found himself in San Francisco, the grizzled wanderer ready to tap back into civilization. As he had done with the Native Americans, he befriended the Chinese community in Chinatown, quickly picking up their language and customs.

James H. Woodall owned an import shop in Chinatown that Gilbert frequented, and had a daughter named Nancy Jane. Her visits to her father's office often coincided with

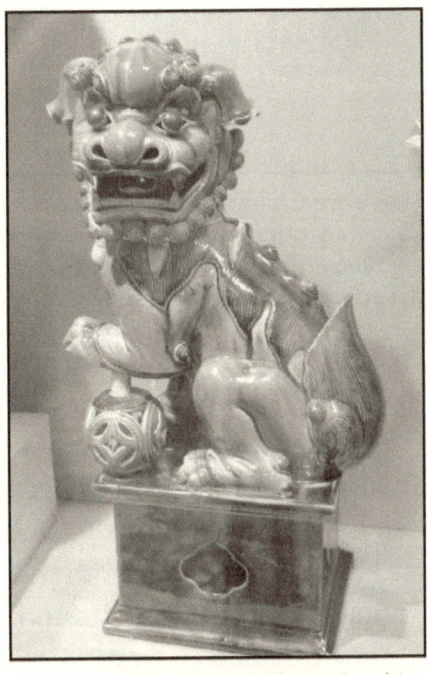

Lion, Qing Dynasty (1644-1911); Chinese; Porcelain

Shortly after arriving in San Francisco in 1897, Gilbert began frequenting a Chinese import shop, owned by James H. Woodall. This figure of a lion was the first thing Gilbert bought there, and on that day, he met Woodall's daughter, Nancy Jane. The two fell in love and were soon married. They were not only partners in life, but also business partners, as they also started importing Chinese art, with Nancy Jane taking care of the stateside portion while Gilbert traveled and sent objects to her. This figure stayed in their home for the rest of their lives, an endearing memento of when they first met.

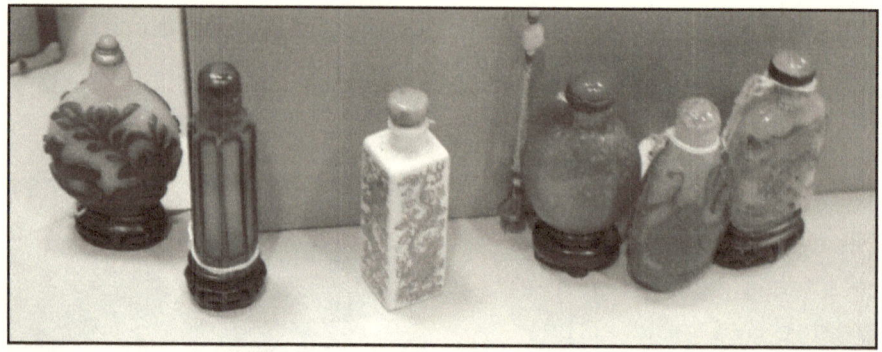

These are Chinese snuff bottles. They're about three inches tall, and delicately decorated, often painted on the inside of the bottle. Gilbert enjoyed collecting them, but there is no substantial evidence to support the rumor that he was involved in the opium trade.

Gilbert's. The two became smitten with each other, and they were soon married.

When Gilbert learned that a trade ship was heading to Shanghai in 1899, he and his new wife saw an opportunity to visit China. He was able to get a job on board, largely due to his ability to converse with the Chinese. The fact that the Boxer Rebellion had recently started only added to his excitement.

They traveled between California and China repeatedly until Nancy Jane became pregnant, after which she remained in Alameda as Gilbert continued traveling. He arranged to be home when Nancy Jane's pregnancy neared term, and on March 13, 1905, she gave birth to twin boys, Benjamin Gilbert and Patrick Gabriel.

Gilbert was out of the country, and Nancy Jane and the year-old twins were fortunately out of town visiting Nancy Jane's mother, when the San Francisco Earthquake hit on April 18, 1906. The boys stayed with their maternal grandmother as Nancy Jane returned to Alameda to retrieve what she could and find new housing for her family. They eventually resettled in Oakland.

Gilbert's passion for the culture resulted in his allegiance to the Chinese during the Boxer Rebellion. That an American would do such a thing was considered scandalous, and Germany and England thought of him as an enemy. However, the Chinese government noted his aid, and he became an unofficial American diplomat during the Xinhai Revolution of 1911, which ended imperial rule in China.

Following the revolution, with his well-established relationship with the Chinese, he began collecting Chinese art and cultural artifacts as a means to protect China's history from the new

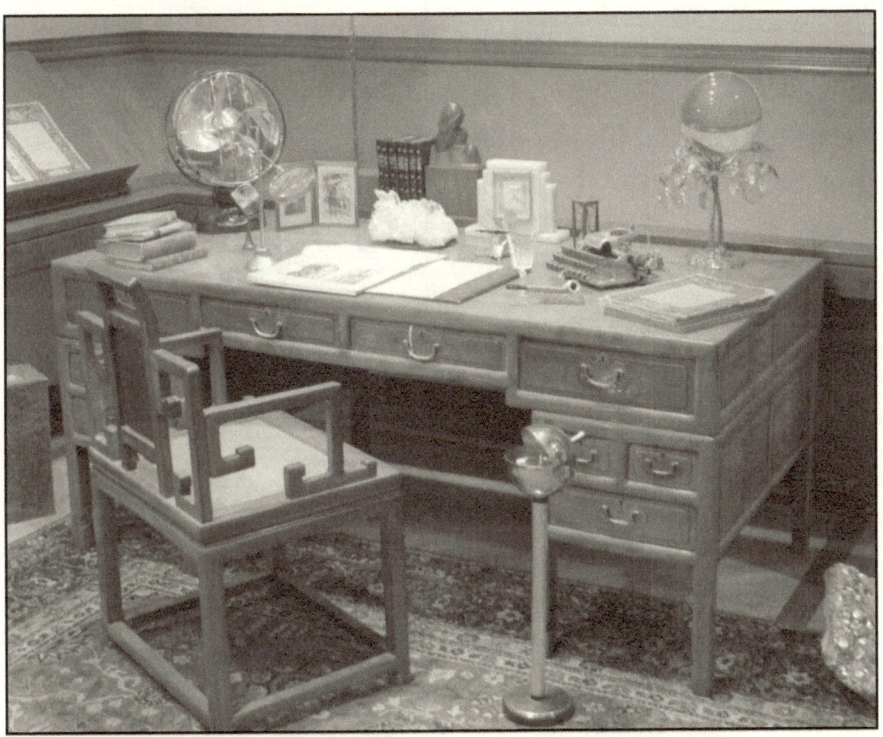

On a trip to Shanghai, this desk immediately captured Gilbert's fancy. Unfortunately, another American, Laurence Sickman, had his eye on it as well. Without delay, Hargrove bought it from under Sickman's nose. More than a decade later, Gilbert's son, Benjamin, worked with Sickman as a Monuments Man after World War II, and Sickman discovered that Gilbert still had the desk. This was a source of much good-natured teasing between the two for several years, as Sickman pretended to make offers on it, and Gilbert refused. When Sickman was made the director of the Nelson in 1953, Gilbert commemorated the event by having the desk delivered to his friend, with a note that teased, "Now stop pestering me. Whining does not befit a museum director."

republic. As an English-speaking authority on China's culture, he was an ambassador to early collectors and archeologists, such as Johan Gunnar Andersson. In fact, Gilbert was on Andersson's excavation site when Peking Man's teeth were first found.

During this time, Gilbert authored several popular books about his travels, but as they were geared toward young readers, they were magnificently embellished with perils, romance, and exotic escapades. The books were actually written by newspaper reporter Ed Spivey, who never ventured far from his assigned base in Shanghai. Spivey was a close friend of Gilbert's and spent many nights listening to him drunkenly boast of his accomplishments. Only the book *Treasures of the Orient,* although a fictional story fraught with melodrama, imparts much of Gilbert's actual knowledge of Chinese antiquities and culture.

The stories of his many adventures in China were later adapted into movie serials and Gilbert is regarded as the inspiration for the character of Indiana Jones. He was even known to carry a whip.

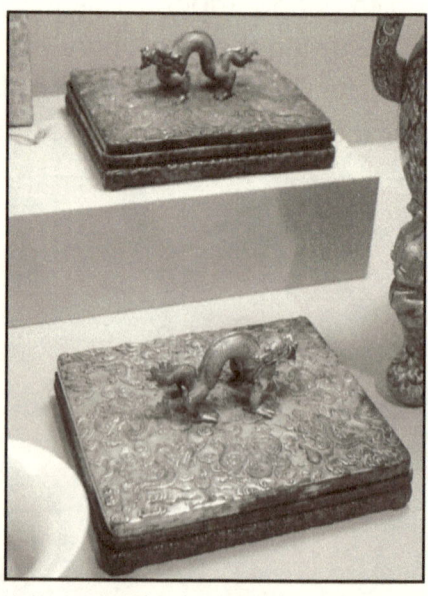

Liu Yong; Imperial Seal, ca. 1748; Gilt copper alloy, wood stand

Liu Yong (1719–1804) was a Chinese politician and calligrapher in the Qing Dynasty. He served in a number of high-level positions with a reputation for being incorruptible, including as the Minister of Rites and Minister of War, and is regarded by some as the "most influential calligrapher of his time." In 1924, Gilbert met with the last emperor of the Qing Dynasty (ended by the Xinhai Revolution), Pu Yi, shortly after he fled Beijing, about purchasing some imperial artifacts. The young monarch was, at the time, so enamored with his new motorcycle that he sold items, including this seal, to Gilbert for very low prices.

One of the adventures that made Gilbert known throughout the world was when he announced in 1919 he would make the first flight over the Himalayas, taking off from Tibet and landing again in India. The stunt garnered headlines around the world and he departed China with much ballyhoo, but never arrived in India. He was presumed dead, until he was discovered a year later working in a remote village. Unable to withstand the high altitude, Gilbert was forced to land on the plateau and nearly starved until he was rescued by nomadic traders. While he was missing, Albert Cushing Reed made the first trans-Atlantic flight. A flight wouldn't be made over the Himalayas until 1933.

Upon his return to Shanghai, Gilbert initiated trade

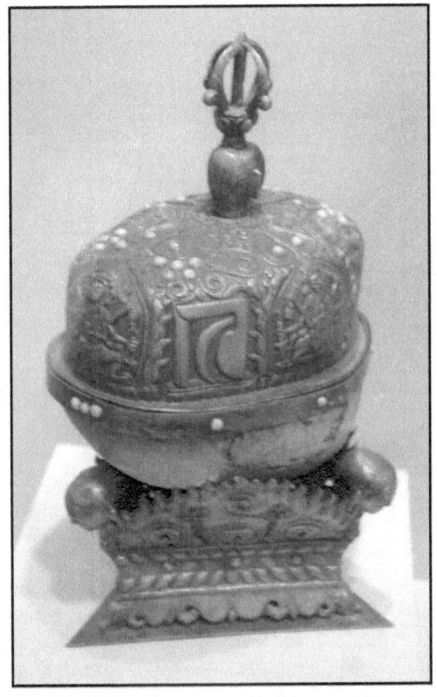

Ceremonial Skull Cup, Cover, and Stand, Late 19th-early 20th century; Tibeto-Chinese; Copper, bone, turquoise

Gilbert secured this ceremonial skull cup toward the beginning of the Xinhai Revolution. It was the first time he'd come in contact with artwork made of human bones, and he was simultaneously sickened and transfixed: "...gruesome to our Western eye, it is not a souvenir of war, but rather a memento of sorts, a revered relic."

with his contacts back in San Francisco, and Nancy Jane acted as liaison with increasing frequency. She quickly became very knowledgeable regarding the conservation of artifacts, and established important contacts in the art world.

Trade began in earnest when he learned from his son, Benjamin, that the soon-to-be-built Nelson Gallery in Kansas City intended to create the first major gallery in America devoted

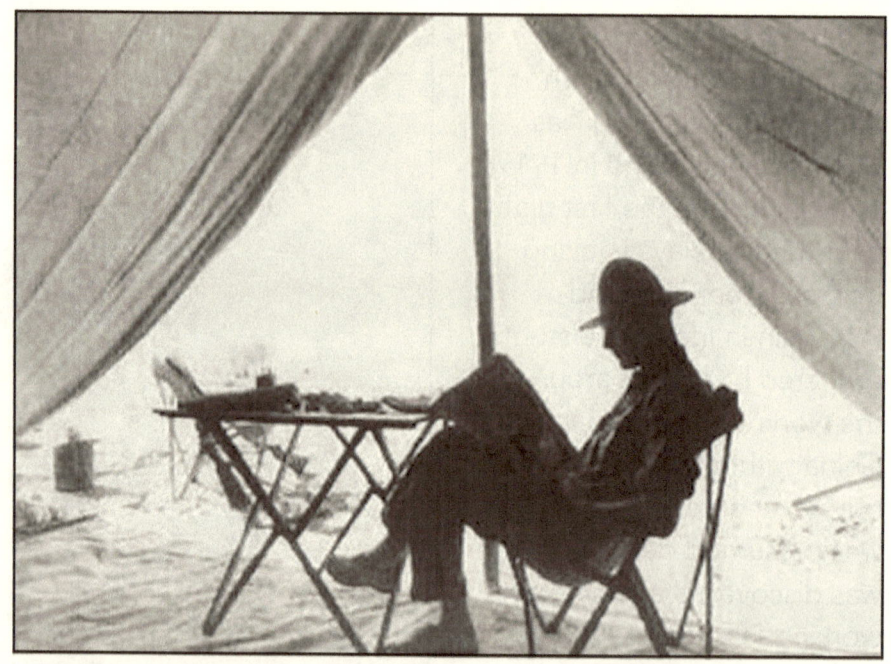

Gilbert Hargrove camping in Mongolia during Johan Gunnar Andersson's famous archeological expedition. Hargrove was the real life inspiration for Indiana Jones.

solely to Chinese art. Gilbert was in the perfect position to help the Nelson in this endeavor, and aided liaison Laurence Sickman in the hunt for precious works of art.

Gilbert traveled to Kansas City for the opening of the Nelson Gallery in 1933. Now 63 years old, Gilbert was not well enough to return to China, but continued as an art dealer in San Francisco.

Gilbert and Nancy Jane soon relocated to Kansas City to oversee the collection that they helped bring to the Nelson. Gilbert was tragically killed in a streetcar accident in the fall of 1940. After her husband's death, Nancy Jane was often found wandering the gallery her husband helped create. Her body was found, slumped on the Gallery's south steps, in 1948. Her obituary stated that "heartbreak finally claimed its victim."

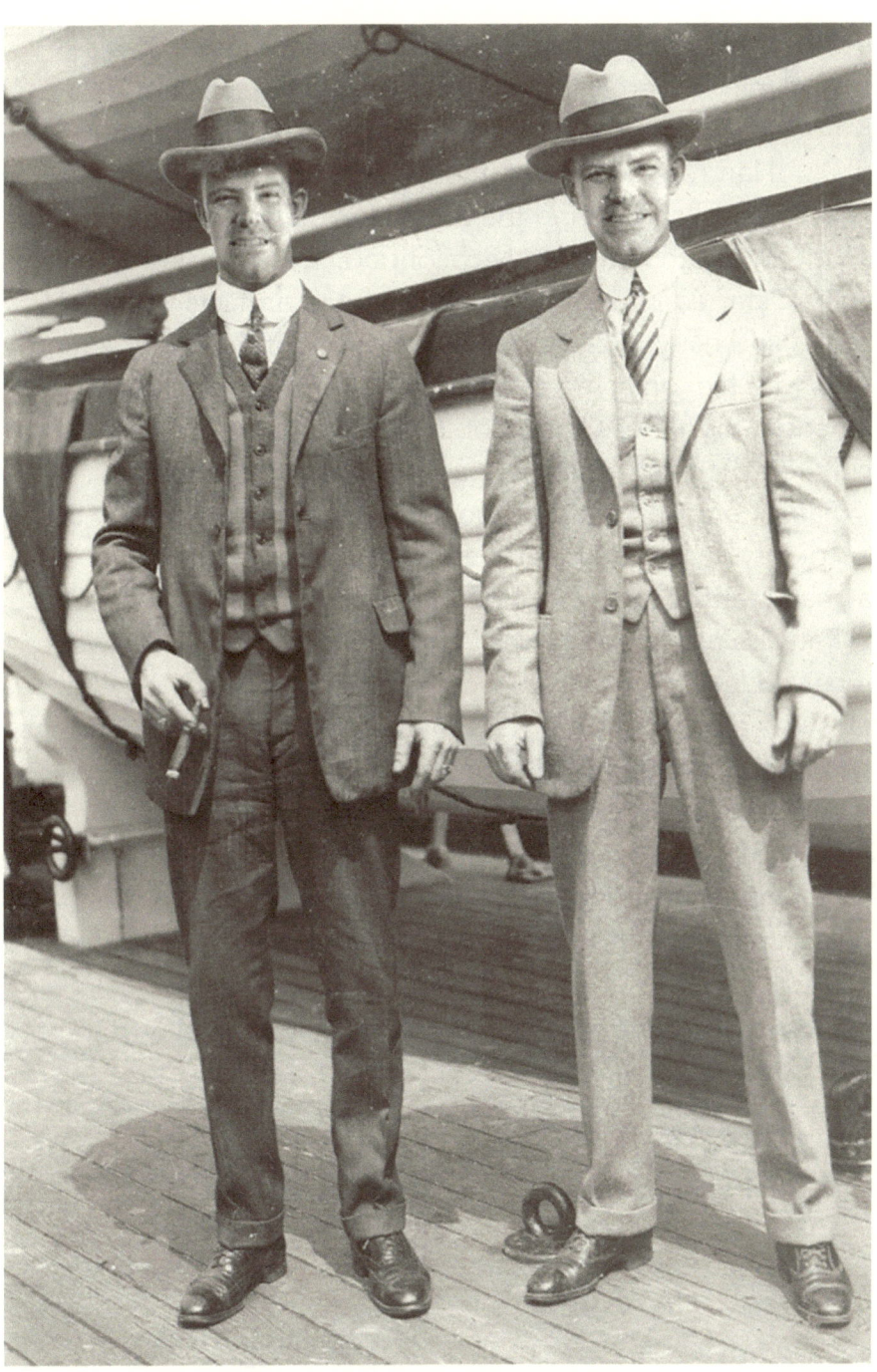

Patrick Hargrove (1905-1947)

Patrick (left) and his twin brother Benajmin on a voyage to China to meet their father in 1929.

Patrick Gabriel Hargrove and his twin brother Benjamin Gilbert Hargrove were born on March 13, 1905 in Alameda, California, to Gilbert and Nancy Jane Hargrove. As their father was an unofficial diplomat in China before and during the Xinhai Revolution, the twins rarely spent time with him in early childhood. This changed when Gilbert started importing Chinese art and artifacts in the late 1910s and early 1920s, and happily brought the eager young men with him on some of his travels. Benjamin obviously inherited his father's knack for immersing himself in another culture, whereas Patrick was fascinated by the art itself.

Patrick enrolled in art school in 1923, at the age of 18. By all accounts, he was eager and enthusiastic, if a bit full of himself, a characteristic thought to be inherited from his famous father.

Patrick's first showing was in his sophomore year. His work received lukewarm praise, mostly for technique. One of his fans was a young art journalist named Marianne Rush, and the two began a romantic relationship.

Although smart and talented, university was difficult for him. A product of the Jazz Age, he often found himself in clubs until early mornings, failing to show up in class the next day. Frequent drunkenness, bursts of violent anger, and

Gilbert Hargrove (1870-1940)

Famed world explorer and art collector who traveled the Old West and China. Inspired the character of Indiana Jones.

Nancy Jane Woodall (1876-1948)

Managed Gilbert's import business in San Francisco and taught her sons the art trade.

Patrick Hargrove (1905-1947)

Art forger who made headlines in the 1930s after his twin brother revealed he was a fraud. He died from alcoholism.

Benjamin Hargrove (1905-1983)

Professional art authenticator who pioneered efforts at art preservation and restoration in post-war America

womanizing also contributed to failing grades. His chronic infidelity put a strain on his relationship with Marianne, and they parted ways less than a year later. After being placed on academic probation for a semester, Patrick was expelled.

For most of the next year, Patrick battled with alcoholism and depression, and attempted suicide at least once, possibly twice. (The vague police report left room for interpretation on the artist's intention.) When a chance meeting with Marianne occurred in the spring of 1927, he quit drinking and resumed studying art, this time on his own.

Patrick immersed himself in the study of early Impressionism. He would work feverishly in his studio for two and three days at a stretch, until exhaustion overcame him.

Using her contacts in journalism, Marianne was able to organize an exhibition of Patrick's new works at the Ghostwriter Gallery in Oakland on August 8, 1930. The night before, Marianne informed Patrick of his impending fatherhood. On the day of the exhibition opening, he wrote in his journal, "The sun rose on this day of beginnings, and I have not arms to embrace it all."

But the exhibition did not go well. Patrick Hargrove's work was uniformly panned as "safe," "restrained," and "derivative." In a rage, Patrick publicly insulted art reviewers, at one point even taking out a newspaper ad in which he ridiculed the appearance of one critic, the sexual proclivity of another, and maligned the parentage of a third. Whatever support he may have once had was lost, and he began drinking again. Marianne tried to get him to focus on preparing for the baby, with limited success. In 1931, their son Rubens Jean-Claude Hargrove was born.

In order to prove to naysayers that he was talented, he began intensely studying—and practicing—the techniques of various Impressionists.

In 1933, as part of an elaborate ruse, Patrick presented his father, now a world-famous art dealer, with a painting he claimed to be by Berthe Morisot but was actually his own forgery. Gilbert seized the work with great gusto and immediately sold it to the Nelson Gallery in Kansas City for $4,000. As a show of gratitude to his son, Gilbert took only 5% commission for the sale.

Having established a fictional connection to the European art world, Patrick continued creating paintings in the style of Morisot, Armand Guillaumin, and Paul Cezanne, and presenting them to his father, as well as various other dealers, to sell. Patrick and Marianne, who was apparently ignorant of the scam, enjoyed a very comfortable lifestyle, and in 1934, had another son, whom they named Titian Salvador.

They planned to marry in early 1939, and a content Patrick got sloppy with his counterfeits. Gerald Washburn, of the Mendenhall Museum, considering the purchase of a newly-discovered Edgar Degas painting entitled *Backstage (Rehearsal)*, called on noted authenticator Benjamin Hargrove, Patrick's twin brother, to verify its legitimacy. When it was discovered

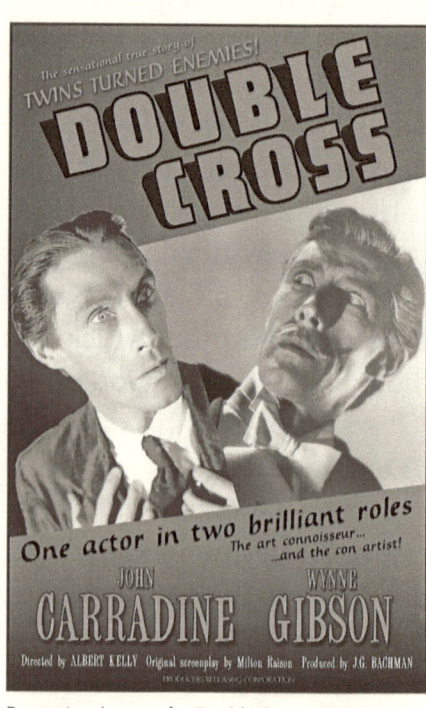

Promotional poster for *Double Cross*, 1941; Directed by Albert Kelly; Producers Releasing Corporation

Double Cross stars John Carradine as both Patrick and Benjamin Hargrove in a film very loosely based on the sensational news story about the twin brothers. The low-budget film's release was overshadowed by the attack on Pearl Harbor, but it is notable for showcasing John Carradine's talent as a painter.

to be a fake, an investigation ensued, and Patrick's chosen occupation was exposed. He was sentenced to two years.

The elder Hargrove was infuriated by the subterfuge, and was forced to spend much time and effort repairing relationships with clients who were now suspicious of the Hargrove name. Benjamin was simultaneously outraged with his brother's deceptions, and wracked with guilt over condemning his nephews to a fatherless life. For the duration of Patrick's sentence, Benjamin supplied Marianne, Rubens, and Titian with a comfortable allowance.

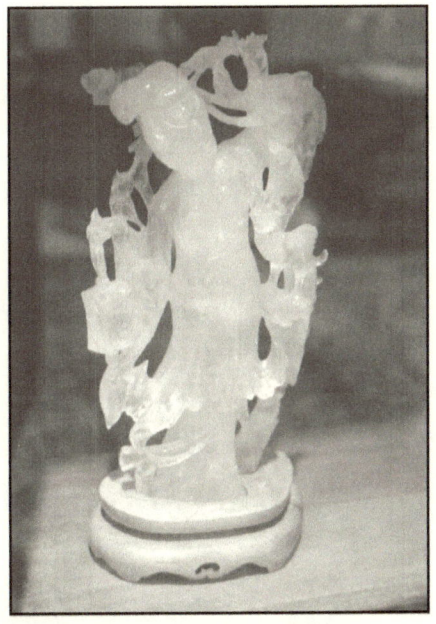

This lovely lady, carved of rose quartz, was the first object that Patrick bought while overseas. He gave it to his mother for her next birthday. When Patrick died, the distraught Nancy Jane carried it for days, cradling it as if it was her own child.

In 1941, B-movie studio Producers Releasing Corporation released *Double Cross*, a movie based on the Hargrove twins' story. John Carradine, himself an artist, played both brothers and created the paintings used in the film.

Patrick was released from prison in 1942. His convict status rendered him ineligible for service in World War II, and he found stable employment painting billboards.

He died of liver disease on February 6, 1947. He was 41.

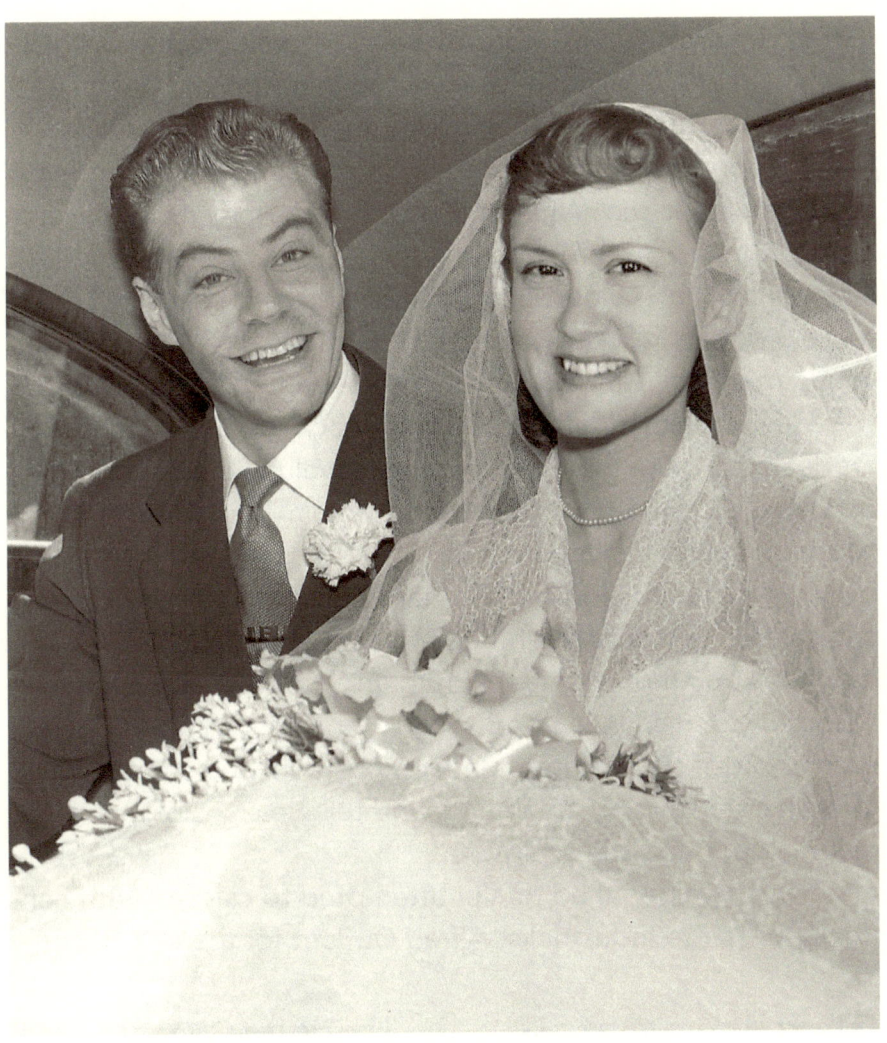

Benjamin Hargrove (1905-1983)

Wedding photo of Benjamin and Flora Hargrove in 1947

Benjamin Gilbert Hargrove and his twin brother, Patrick Gabriel Hargrove, were raised in a world of Chinese art. Throughout their youth, their mother received objects from overseas and negotiated sales with dealers in San Francisco. When they were older, they made several trips to China with their father.

It was through Gilbert that Benjamin met art collector Laurence Sickman in Shanghai in 1931. Close in age, the two young men hit it off, and Sickman showed Benjamin how he was able to gain admittance into the back rooms of Chinese art dealers, where they kept their most valuable artifacts.

Having received his art history degree in 1928, Benjamin kept records for his father's business and continued his studies by seeking mentorship with Bernard Berenson, a leading art critic and collector of the time. While he eschewed Berenson's emphasis on emotional reaction to an art object as evidence of forgery, Benjamin learned to look for artists' "fingerprints" such as brush strokes, pigment composition, and canvas texture when examining a painting, and telltale signs of modern materials and tools in sculpture.

When an unidentified dealer attempted to sell an "18th century" portrait to industrialist Alfred DuPont for the exorbitant

Gilbert Hargrove (1870-1940)

Famed world explorer and art collector who traveled the Old West and China.

Nancy Jane Woodall (1876-1948)

Managed Gilbert's import business in San Francisco and taught her sons the art trade.

Patrick Hargrove (1905-1947)

Art forger who made headlines in the 1930s after his twin brother revealed he was a fraud. He died from alcoholism.

Benjamin Hargrove (1905-1983)

Professional art authenticator who pioneered efforts at art preservation and restoration in post-war America

price of $25,000, Benjamin accompanied curator Arthur Simons to the scene. As Simons expressed suspicion on the painting's authenticity, the price dropped to $10,000, and then to $1,000. Benjamin suggested, and Simons concurred, that it showed signs of overpainting, but agreed with DuPont that the frame itself was worth several hundred dollars, so it was purchased. When the forged overpainting was removed, it was discovered that it had been covering up *Madonna and Child*

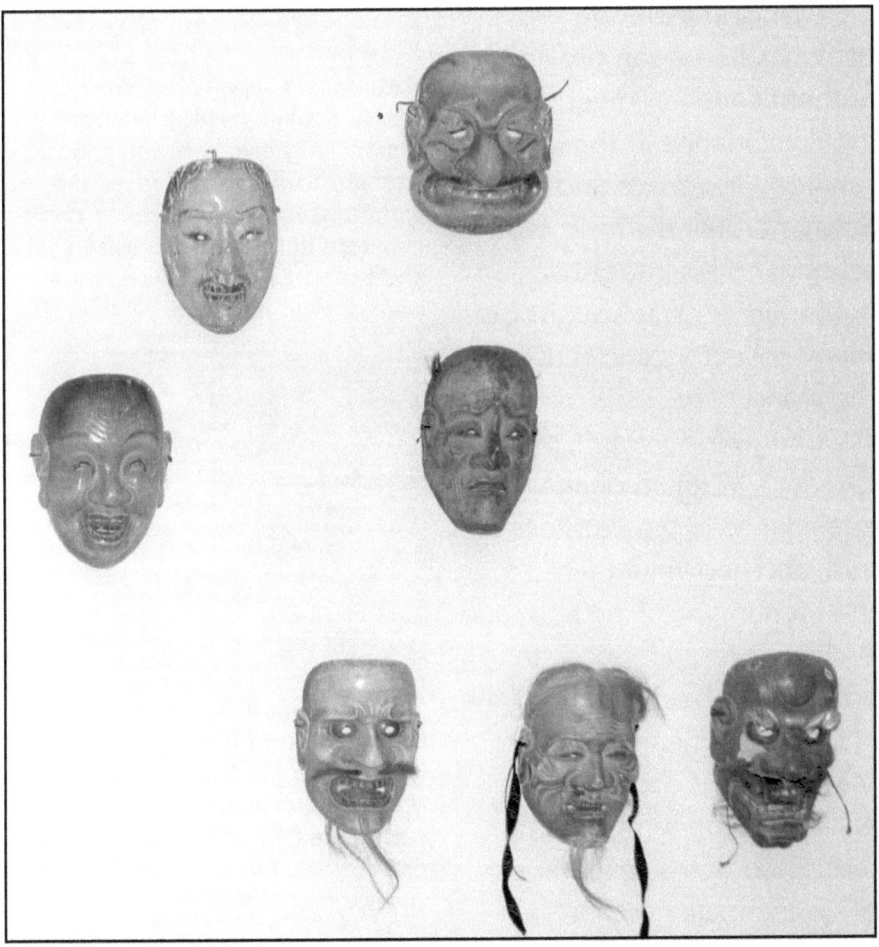

Benjamin Hargrove returned from World War II with many examples of Noh theatre masks.

by Baroque painter Bartolomé Esteban Murillo, valued at $150,000.

Intrigued by this turn of events, Benjamin threw himself into the business of authentication. Having inherited his father's eye for art, this was a field for which he had particular talent. His increasing knowledge proved useful as he began providing authentication and verifying provenance at the newly renamed Hargrove and Son. Soon, he built a strong reputation, and his integrity as an authenticator was sought by many collectors and museums the world over.

During World War II, Major Laurence Sickman dealt with intelligence in the Pacific theatre, and had volunteered for the Monuments, Fine Arts, and Archives program, recovering art that had been stolen by the Nazi Party. When he learned that Benjamin Hargrove had enlisted in the army, Sickman requested him as a member of his team, along with Sherman Lee and Patrick Lennox Tierney, working at General

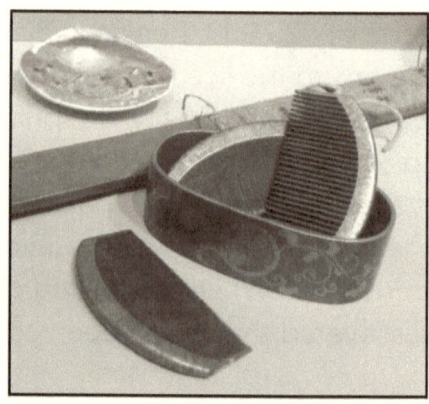

Comb Box with Three Combs, 1800-1850; Japanese; Lacquer with makie (scattered gold leaf) on a nashiji (pear skin) ground; ivory and tortoise shell hair arrangers

Stationed in Japan after World War II, Benjamin Hargrove became romantically involved with a local woman, Yoshiko Ariki. After she went missing, a heartbroken Benjamin kept her antique tortoise shell and ivory hair combs, as a keepsake of their romance.

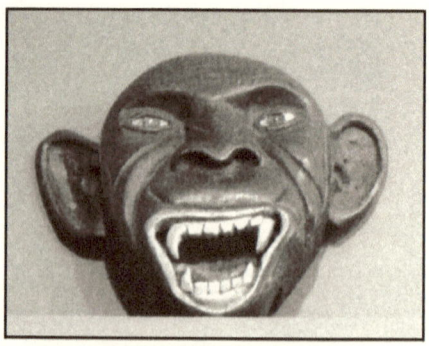

On March 2, 1933, Benjamin Hargrove attended the premiere of *King Kong* in New York City. A collector of masks, Benjamin was thrilled when he received this promotional monkey mask at the theatre that night.

MacArthur's headquarters in Tokyo. His further authentication experience proved a valuable resource—and commodity—when he returned to the United States after the war.

1947 was a very full and emotional year for Benjamin. In January, he married longtime sweetheart Flora Torres. The following month, his estranged twin brother, Patrick, died of liver disease, caused by a lifetime of alcoholism. In October, Benjamin traveled to Amsterdam to testify in the trial of Dutch art forger Han van Meegeren, and in December, his first child, Roger, was born. (The couple had two more children: Violet, in 1948, and Rose, in 1950.)

Benjamin, now well-known in the world of art authentication and conservation, published his 1950 book, *Framing the Dark: The Shadowy World of Art Forgery*. In it, he wrote about a wide range of his experience with forgeries, but since it was the first time he'd ever spoken publicly about his involvement in his brother's conviction, it garnered a flurry of media attention for this alone.

Throughout the 1950s and 60s, Benjamin became a consultant and advised museums in the practices of art conservation and restoration. His work frequently took him to Europe, and he often traveled for pleasure to Africa and South America, where he

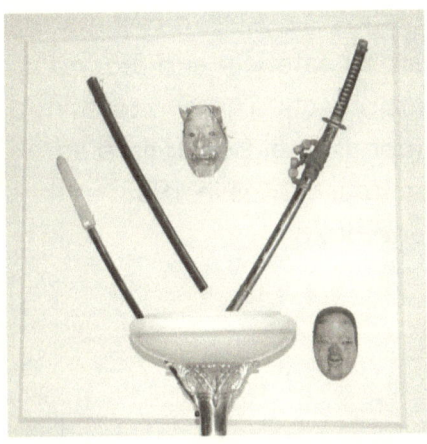

Yamato Daijo, Japanese; Samurai Sword (katana type), Late 18th-early 19th century; lacquered with aogai (mother-of-pearl). Blade is tempered steel

Long sword (tachi) with scabbard, 19th century; Japanese; steel, wood, lacquer.

On the left is a katana, and on the right is a tachi, with its scabbard. These were given to the Twins, Benjamin and Patrick, when they were teens, from a friend of Gilbert's. Nancy Jane, concerned for the boys' safety, immediately locked them away. The twins "liberated" the swords one day, and the following events resulted in a definitive way to tell them apart: a nasty scar on Patrick's left arm.

continued collecting masks and other artifacts from various cultures.

When his old friend Laurence Sickman was appointed director of the Nelson Gallery of Art in 1953, Benjamin attended the ceremony. In the mid-1970s, Benjamin introduced Sickman to the Oddy test, a conservation technique used to test materials for safety in and around art objects. The two remained friends until Benjamin died of natural causes in 1983, at the age of 78.

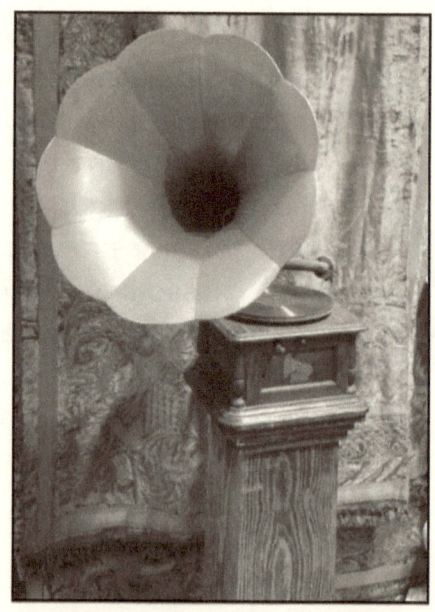

This phonograph was at Grandpa Ben and Grandma Flora's house. I was quite fascinated by it when we visited them when I was a child. It was something of a ritual, because Grandma Flora would only play it after we were sitting quietly, because she was afraid we'd knock into it. Grandpa Ben, though, had me stand on his feet and he danced me around the room.

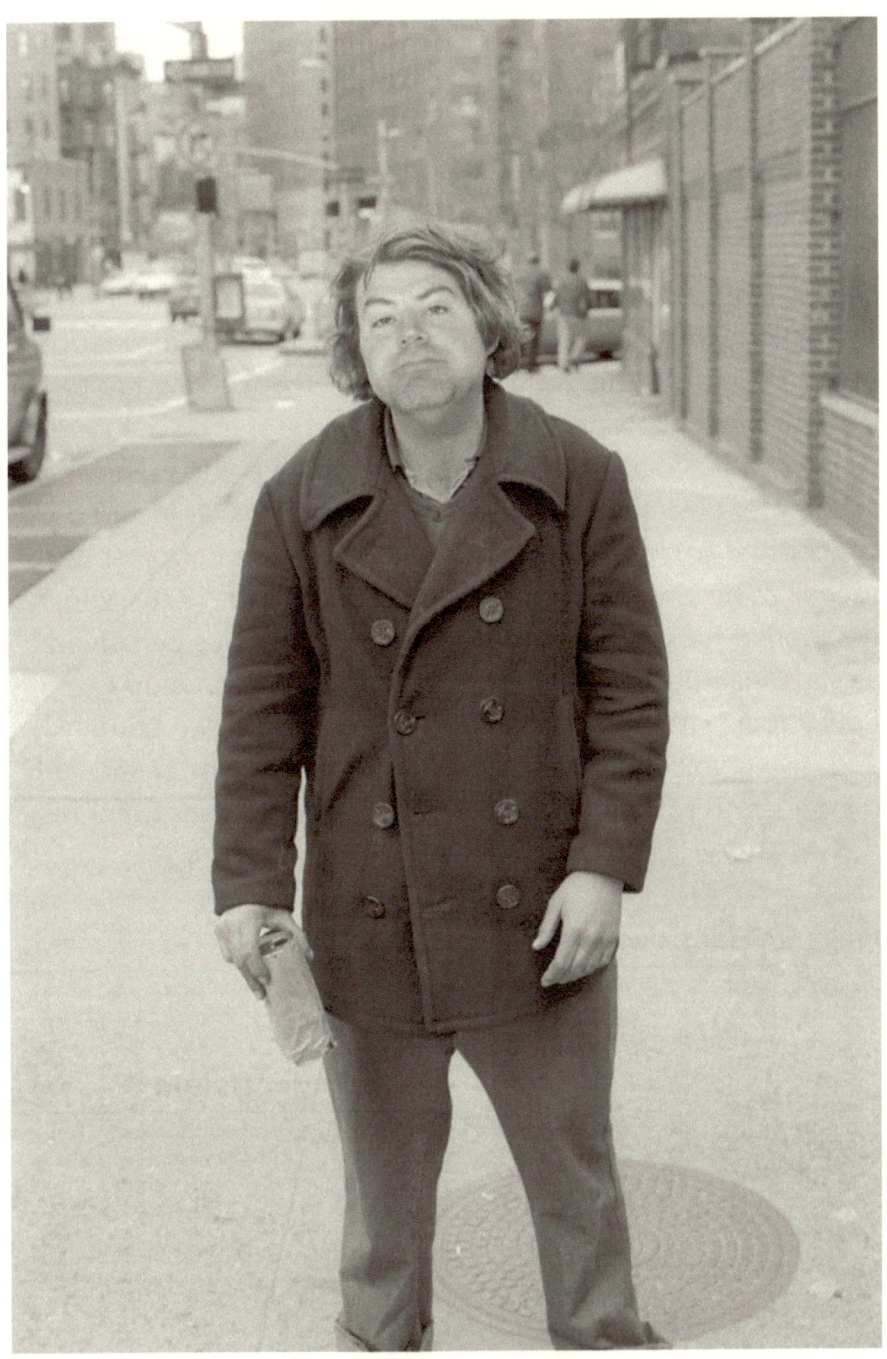

Roger Hargrove (b. 1947)

Portrait taken in New York City in 1986.

The son of art authenticator Benjamin Hargrove, Roger studied philosophy at the University of California in Berkeley during the cultural revolution of the 1960s and became a campus activist. He participated in the anti-war movement helping to organize sit-ins and marching on the Berkeley Draft Board. In the early 1970s, Roger had two children with his first wife, Ginger Abrams.

Thanks to his father's work, Roger gained some knowledge of the art world in his youth and applied that knowledge to his activism. Following the Vietnam War, he started the journal *No Art*, which focused on institutional critique and advocated for greater diversity in museum exhibition. He was inspired by conceptual artists like Michael Asher and Allen Ruppersberg as well as his own family history. Published from 1978-1986, the journal took a radical stance against what was perceived as staid institutionalism in the art world and advocated a "punk rock" attitude toward culture – tearing down barriers and giving voice to artists outside the mainstream, particularly minorities. Throughout his career, Roger was criticized for his

Benjamin Hargrove (1905-1983)

Professional art authenticator who pioneered efforts at art preservation and restoration in post-war America

Flora Torres (1922-2005)

Music prodigy who played violin for the San Francisco Symphony.

Roger Hargrove (b. 1947)

Activist who pushed for diversity in museums and now advocates for the indigenous Northwest people.

Violet Hargrove (b. 1948)

Studied dance before marrying and settling in Butte, Montana.

Rose Hargrove (b. 1950)

Spent 25 years as an arts educator in Chicago.

anti-elitist stance because he was the grandson of the famous Gilbert Hargrove, even though his father Benjamin had long ago stopped supporting him because of his anti-war activities in the 1960s.

Neglectful of his own family, Roger divorced in 1982 and Ginger, a secretary for the Southern Pacific Railroad in Burlingame, moved with their two children to work at GTE Sprint in Kansas City. Roger found himself on a fast downward spiral fueled by drugs and investments in controversial and costly conceptual art exhibitions.

One of the more notable exhibits that Roger sponsored featured the paint brushes, clothing, tools, and other personal items of famous artists, but none of their art. He wrote in *No Art* that "people who like relics get excited, not about the saint, but about the saint's bones. What they want from artists is not the art but the button torn from their jacket."

He also financed the notorious artist Joan Mundy, who would purchase art from galleries and then add her own embellishments to the work. Roger defended her, saying she had as much right to creative input as the artist that originally painted the piece, but the arts community loudly denounced her as a vandal and defacer of great art. There was little they could do, however, since she owned the works in question.

After Mundy's creative enhancements to a painting by Millet, action was taken to stop her. Her appearance at auction houses and galleries caused intense bidding wars as collectors sought to keep art out of her destructive hands. Mundy was priced out of the market and eventually banned from Sotheby's. She sued Sotheby's, but died in an automobile accident before the trial could take place. Ironically, some of the works of art "defaced" by Joan Mundy are worth considerably more today thanks to her alterations. The Millet painting recently sold for $1.3 million.

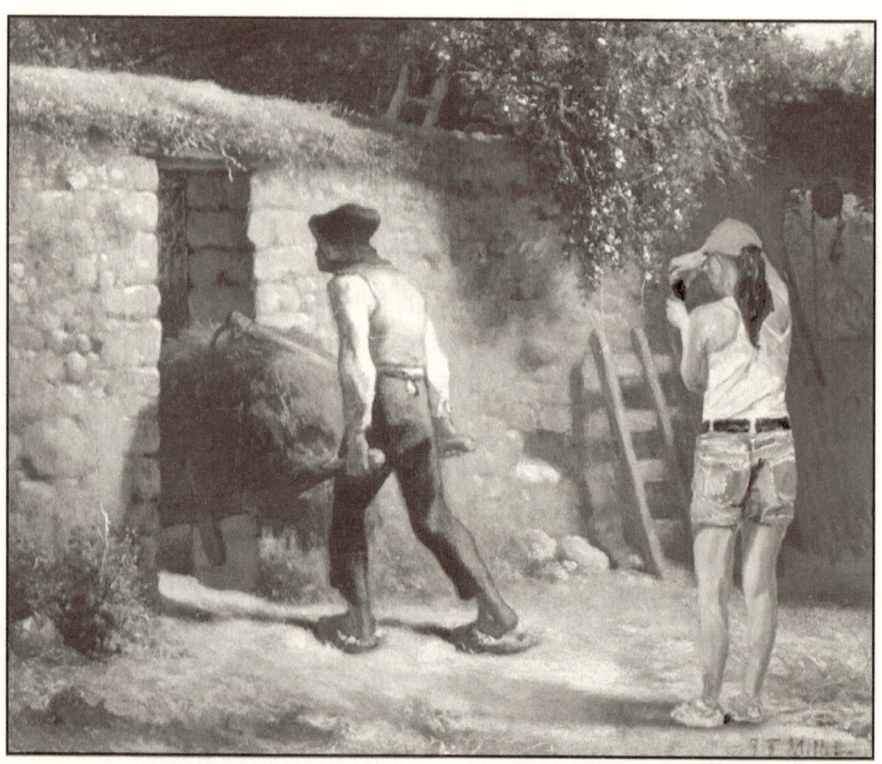

Artist Joan Mundy became infamous when she painted over this rustic painting by Jean-Francois Millet, adding a woman photographing the farmer as he pushes his wheelbarrow through a doorway. Roger Hargrove wrote in *No Art*, "While Millet painstakingly captured this realistic scene with oil paints, Mundy's tourist captures it in an instant on film with her camera... she at once questions the need for realistic art and devalues Millet's work as simply old world kitsch." Despite the outcry Mundy's alteration originally caused, when an art restoration expert offered to try and remove Mundy's handiwork in 2006, there was an equally voluminous demand to leave it as it was.

Roger Hargrove's downfall came in 1985 after a national outcry over an exhibit at the Charleston Museum in South Carolina of tombstones taken from an abandoned Civil War graveyard. Condemned for disrespecting the dead, Roger countered that it was the same sort of grave robbing that Native Americans had been complaining about for decades. As Roger explained, "Today's museums are no better than the tombs they raided. These modern mausoleums worshiping dead culture are just that – death cults." The controversy was fueled by the fact that Roger had received partial funding for the exhibit, in the amount of $1,000, from the National Endowment for the Arts. It was unfortunately the death knell for *No Art*, which lost its backers and advertisers, as well as its influence.

Roger's frequent complaints against museums was that "history shows us that artists starve and suffer in their lifetimes only to be celebrated as great geniuses after they're dead, yet today's museum culture carries on this tradition. We should be celebrating those geniuses who are still alive and yearning to be heard." He called museums places "where art goes to die" and advocated for more fine art in public spaces – the office, the shopping mall, the nightclub, the gas station, the public restroom. "Art must be a daily part of our lives. It needs to be woven into the fabric

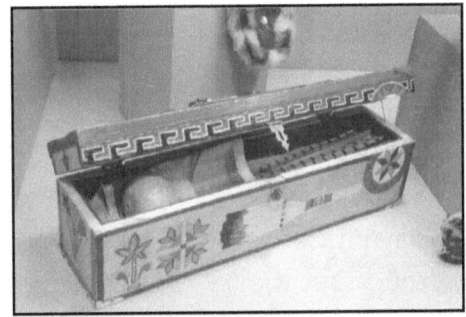

Peyote Box, ca. 1950; Navajo; wood, pigment, silver, brass, felt, ferrous metal, and rhinestones

This is the peyote box that my dad, Roger, used to carry his "ceremonial" supplies. Emptied of his belongings, it made an awesome jewelry box for me in college.

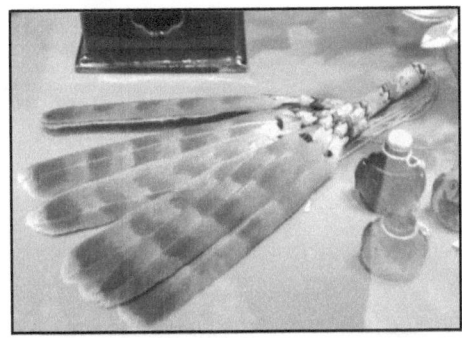

Peyote Fan, ca. 1920; Plains; twelve hawk feathers (full tail), turkey (?) feathers, native leather, glass and brass beads, and German silver

When Roger and his first wife, Ginger, started dating, she gave him this fan to use for his own bastardization of peyote "rituals." When Ginger left him and moved to Kansas City, she took the fan with her. This upset Roger for awhile, until he decided to quit drug use. Their son, Bryan, used it to dry Dungeons and Dragon miniatures that he painted when he was in high school.

of society, not cloistered away for study. It should be a normal part of our existence, and it should constantly challenge our assumptions."

Following a stint in drug rehab, Roger moved to Seattle in 1989 and married artist Lucy Fontenot, who was known for her avant garde performance art and attacking the status quo. Throughout the 1990s they operated the Font Gallery, a cornerstone of the Seattle arts scene. Roger's primary passion over the last twenty years, following the passing of the Native American Graves Protection and Repatriation Act in 1990, has been working to return works of art to coastal tribe native organizations in Washington and British Columbia.

Exhibit Photos

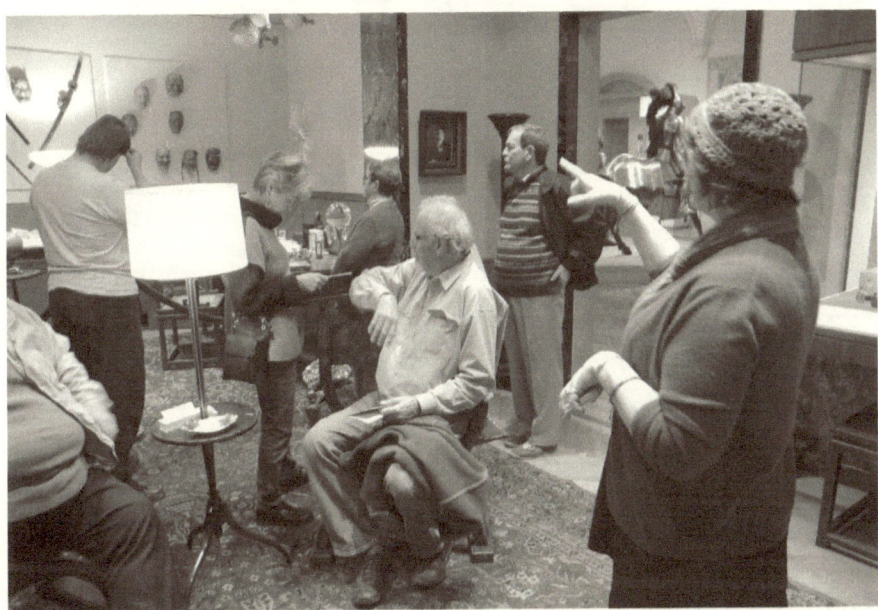

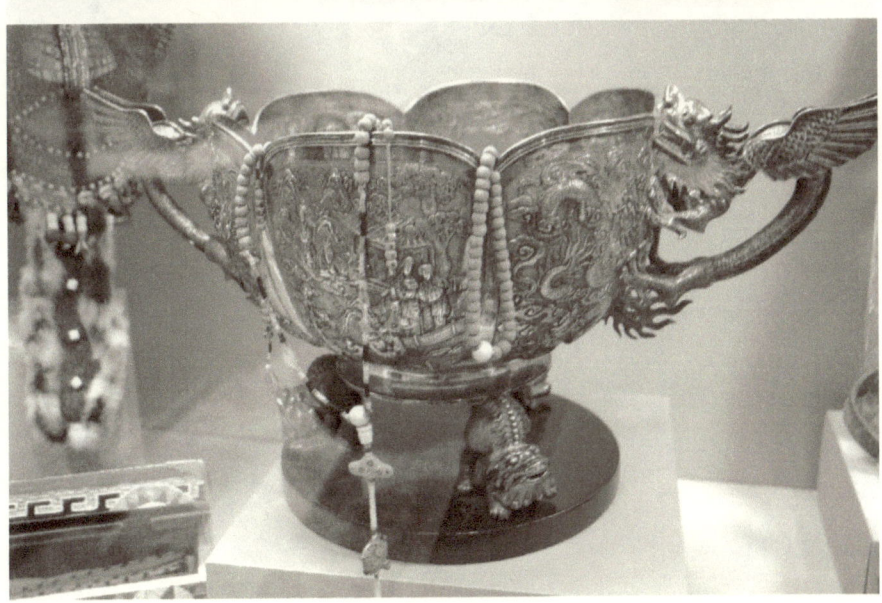

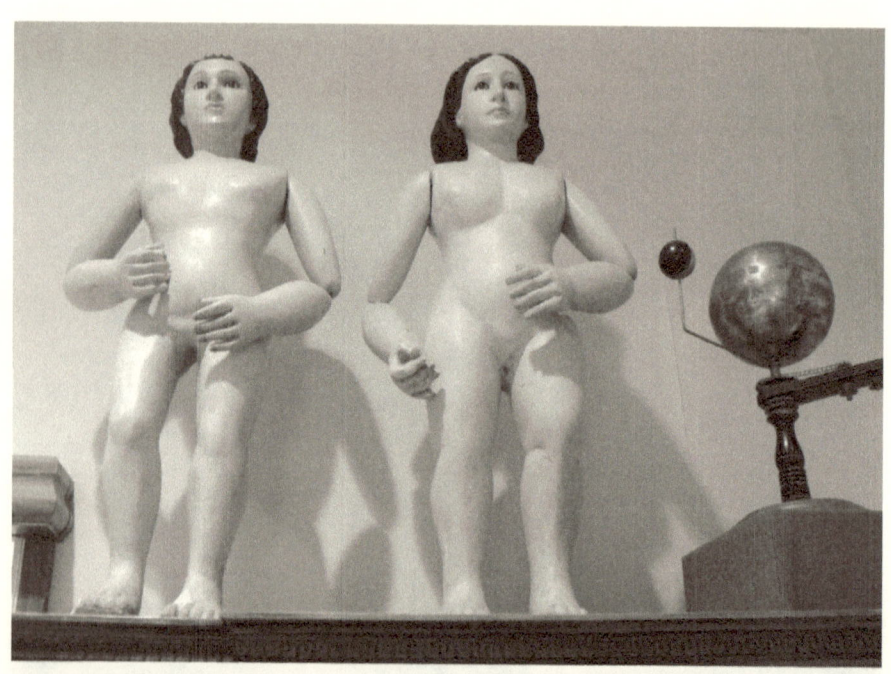

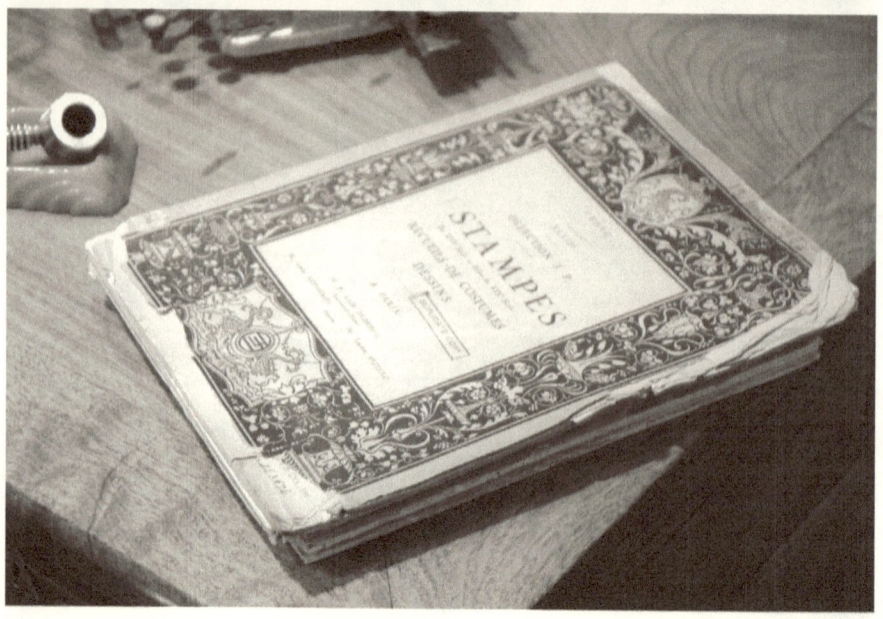

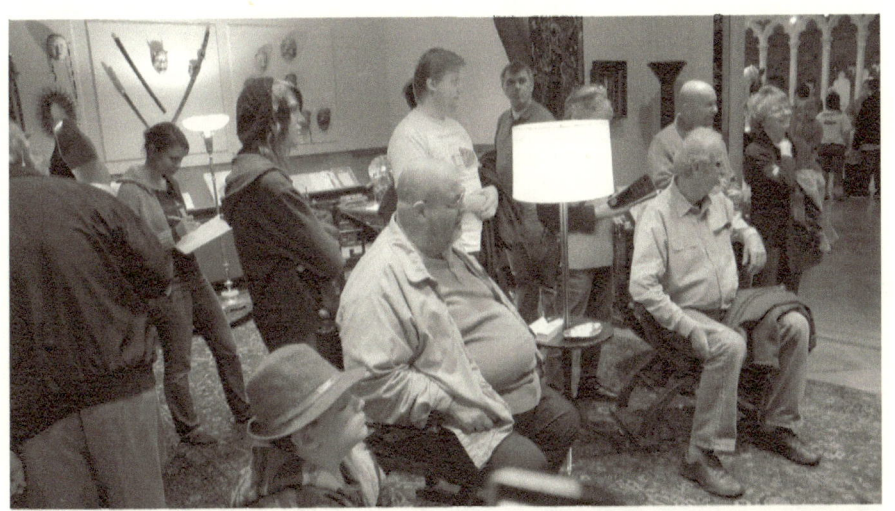

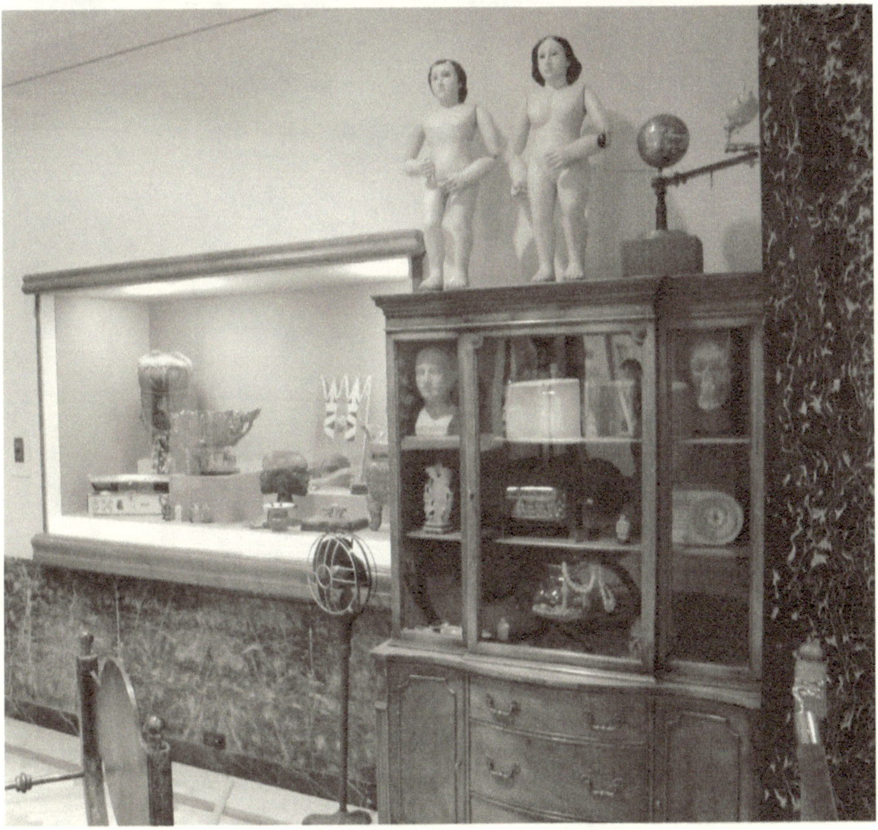

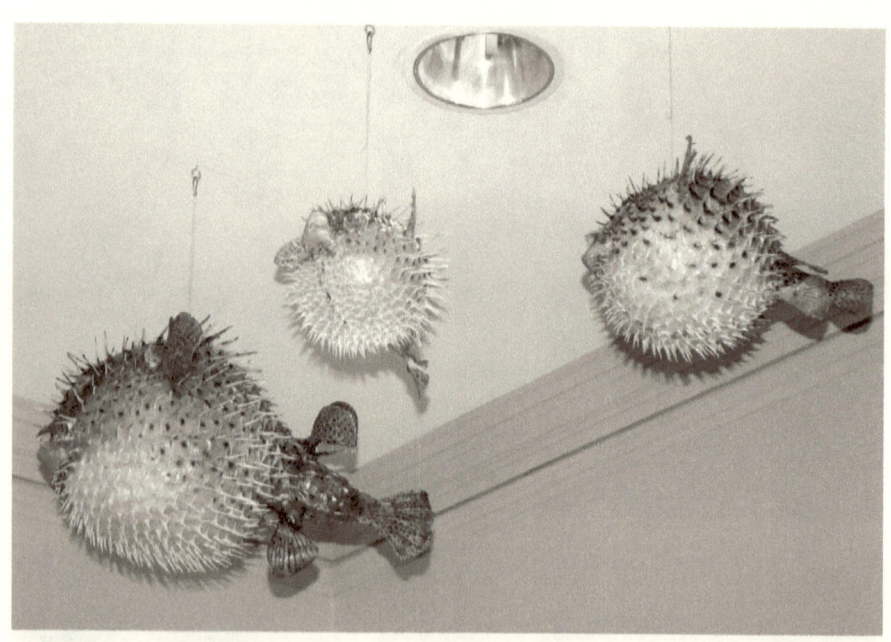

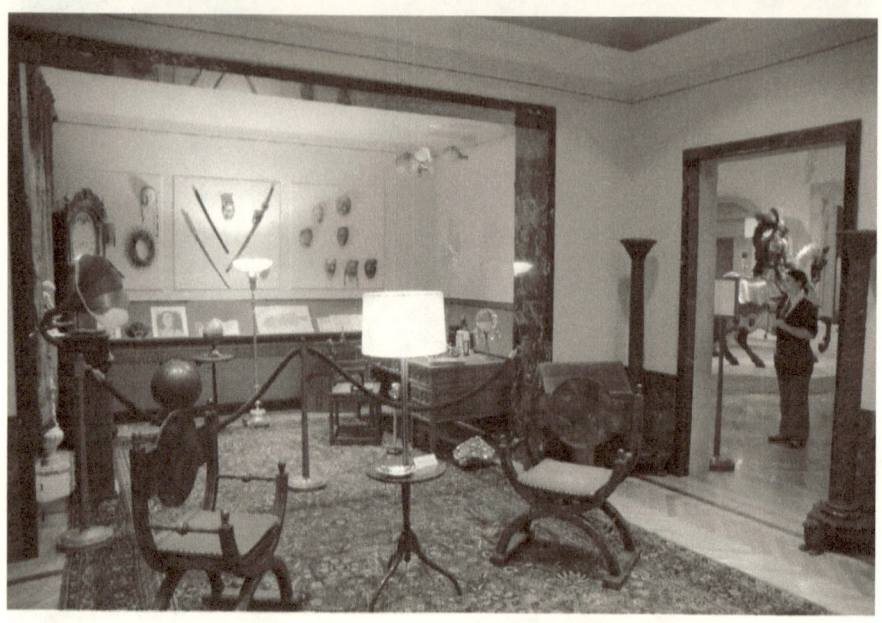

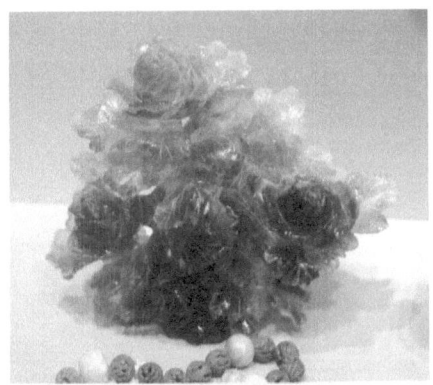

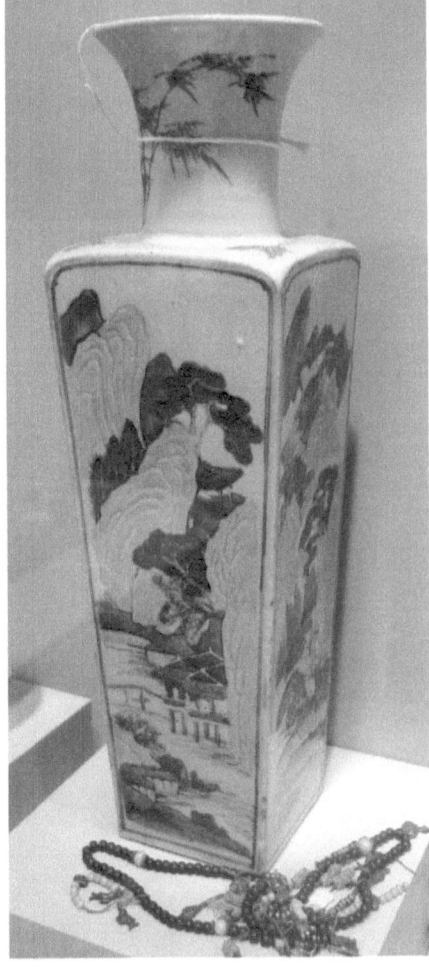

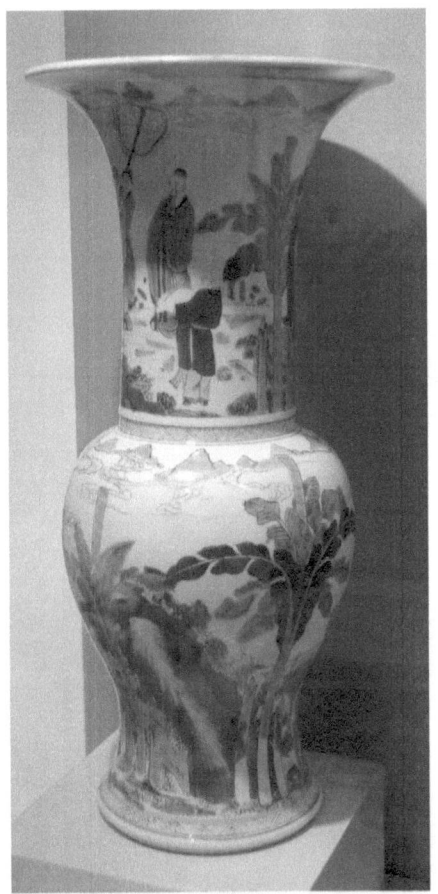

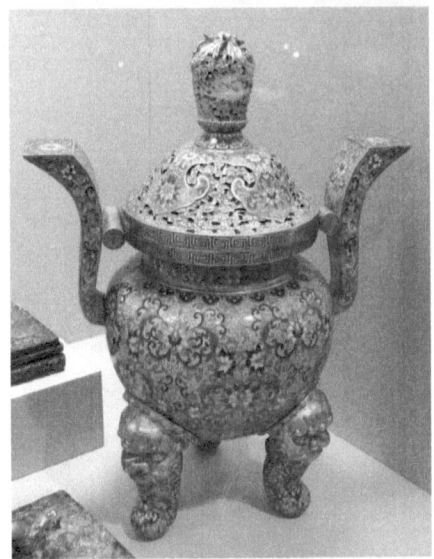

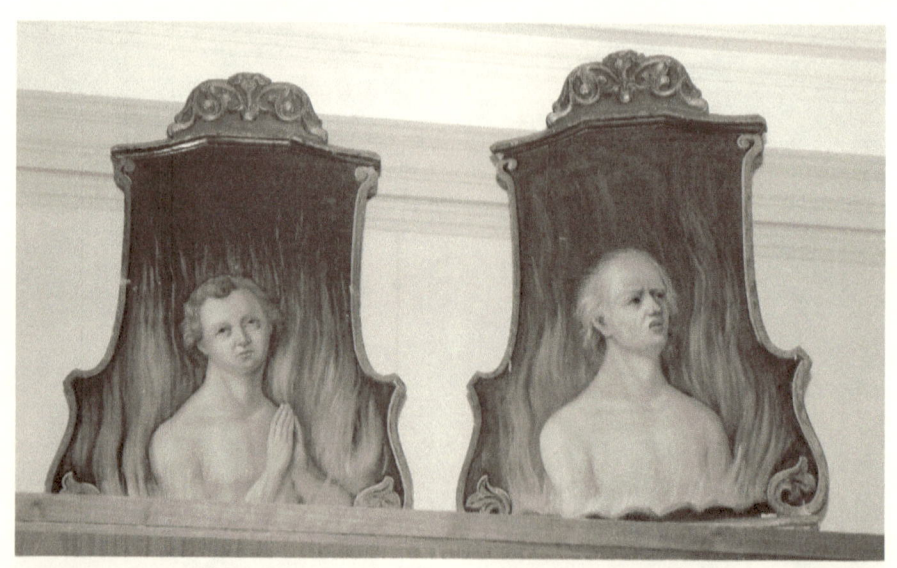

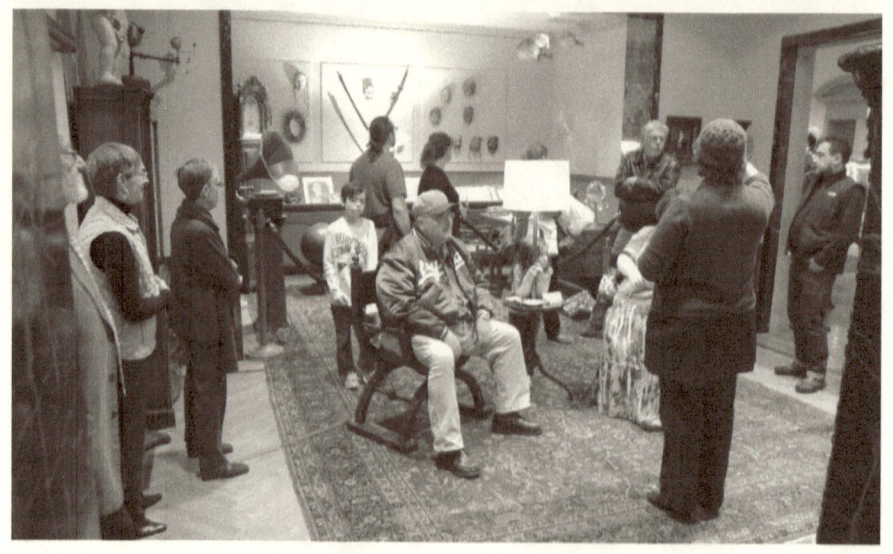

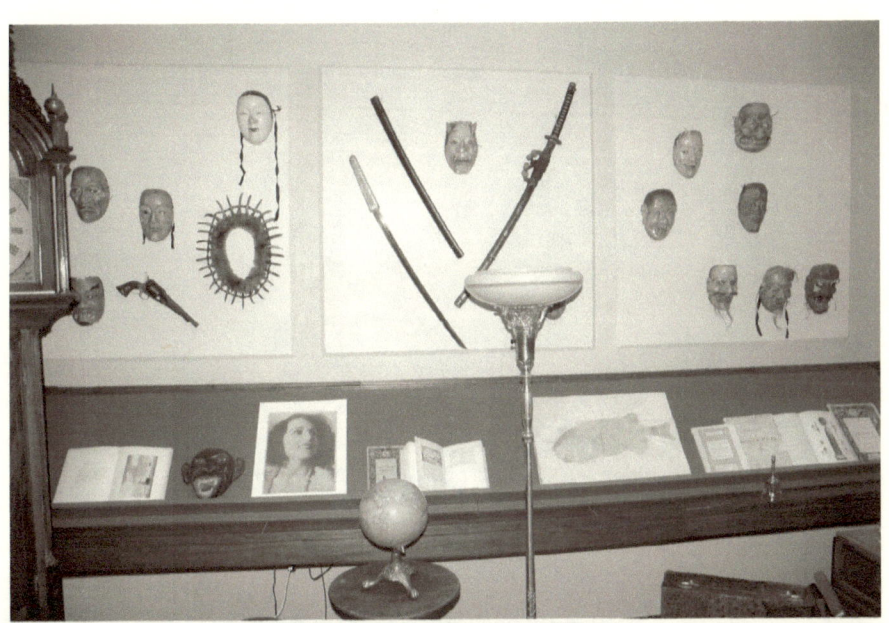

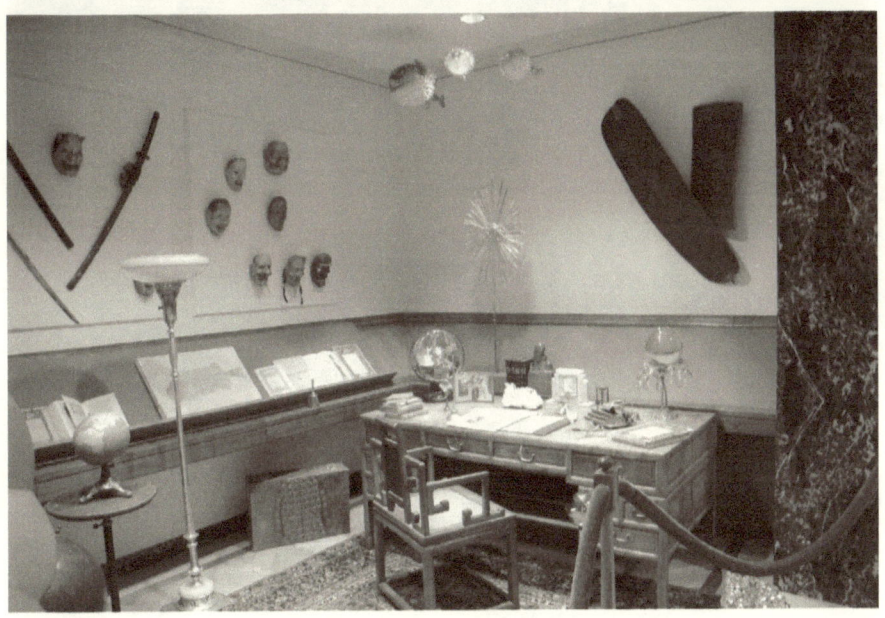

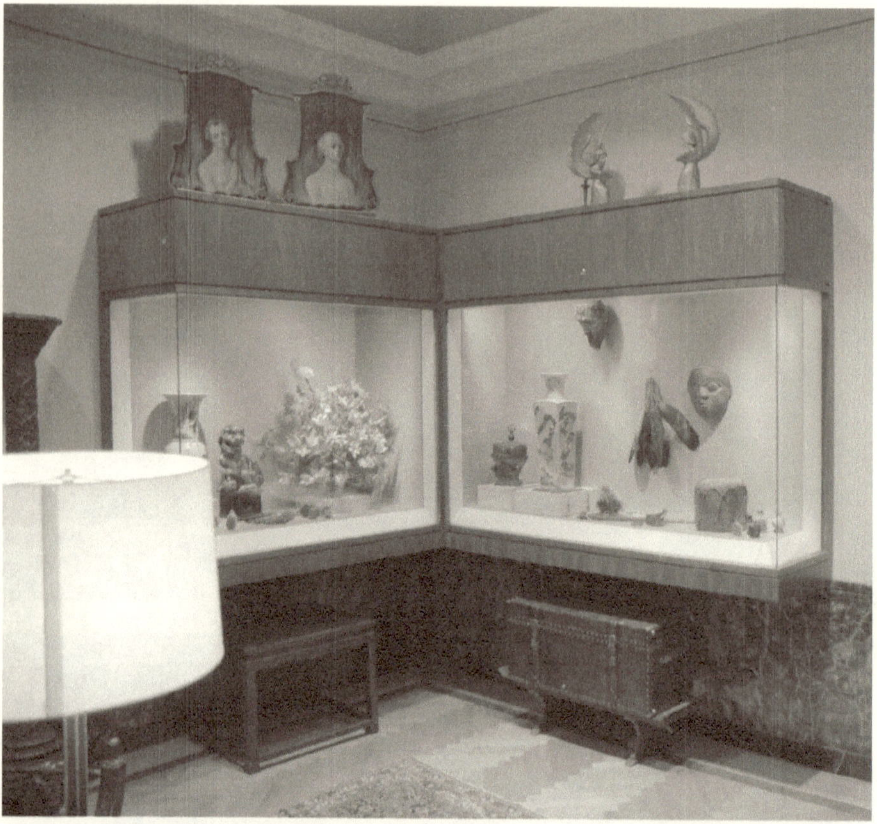

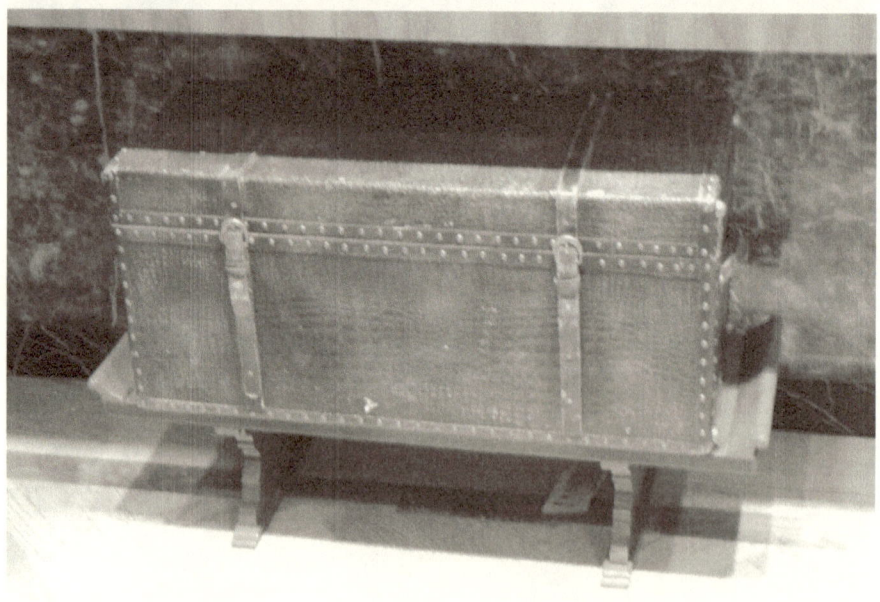

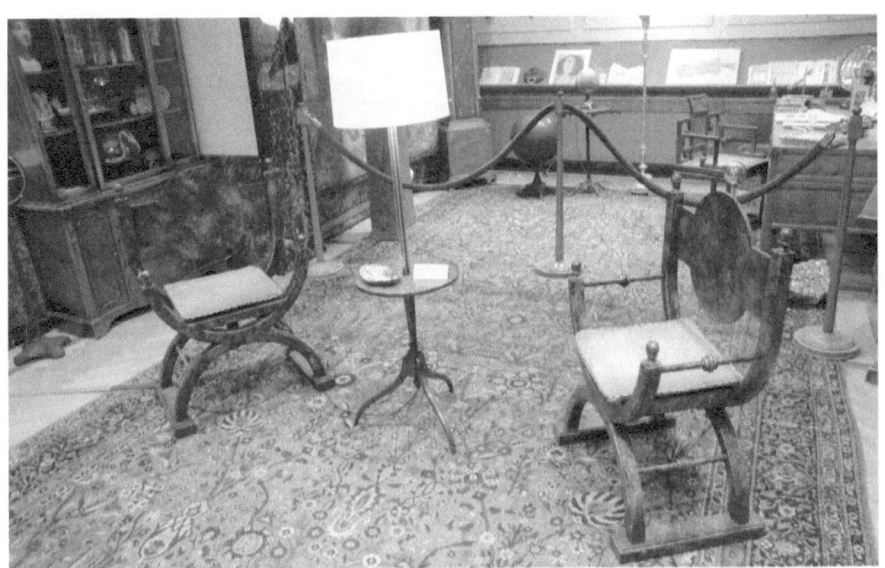

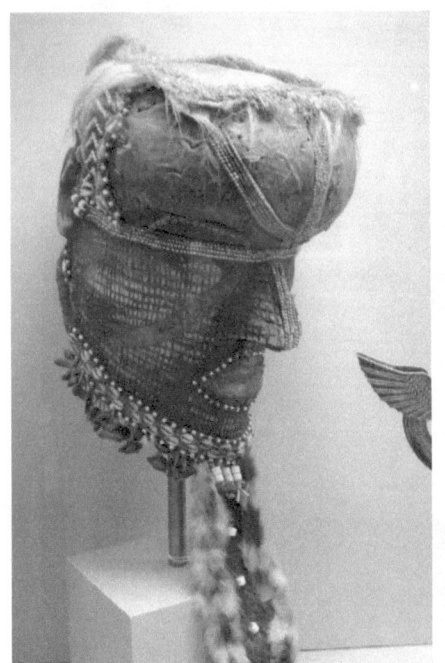

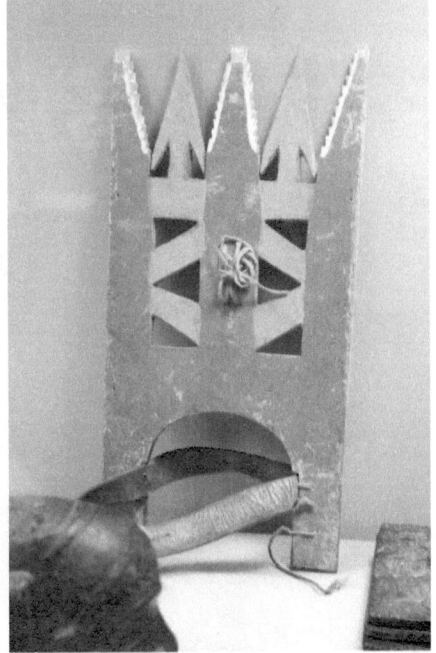

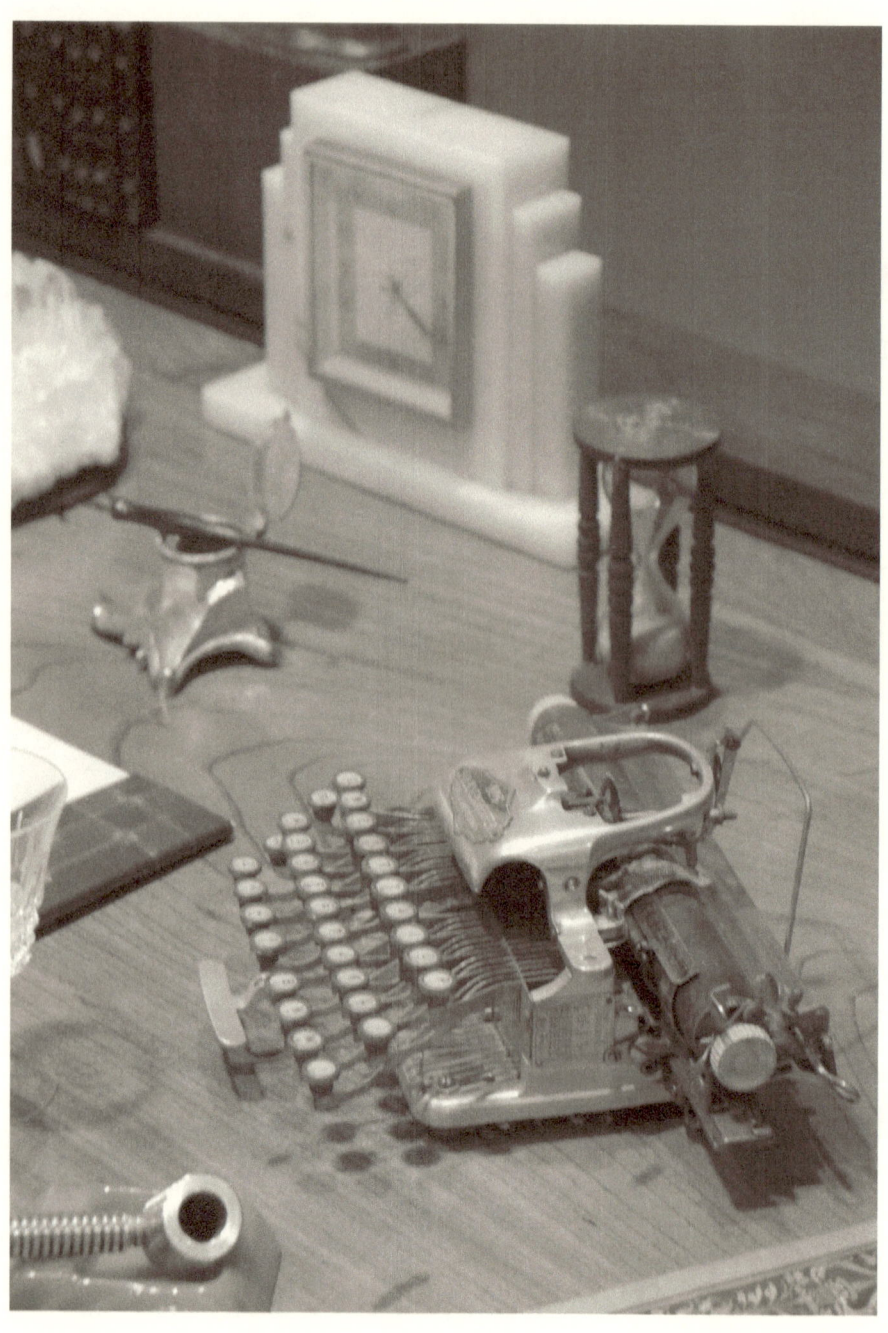

Faking It: Real Stuff, Fictitious Collectors

by Terry Pitts

Reprinted with permission from http://sebald.wordpress.com/2013/02/01/faking-it/

I had just finished making my way slowly more or less chronologically through the galleries of Roman, Greek, Egyptian, and medieval European art at the Nelson-Atkins Museum of Art in Kansas City when I turned a corner into a tiny gallery that appeared to be an exact recreation of someone's study. Judging by the evidence, the time was more or less a century ago and the occupant had clearly been a world traveler, an obsessive collector, and something of an eccentric. The clock in the corner was ticking and it appeared that someone had only moments before slid the chair back from the desk with its ancient typewriter and had walked out into the museum. The introductory panel told me I was looking at "The Magnificent Collection of Gilbert G. Hargrove."

> This installation showcases the collection of Gilbert G. Hargrove and the Hargrove family. Gilbert was born in the sleepy town of Pike Pepper, Ohio in 1870. From an early age, Gilbert was an avid reader, spending hours at the local library pouring over books on history, geography, anthropology and art.
>
> At the age of 16, he left home in search of adventure. His travels led him to Kansas City where he landed a job writing obituaries for *The Kansas City Times*. Suffering from a chronic case of wanderlust, he soon grew restless and headed west. He traveled as far as San Francisco, fell in love and married the daughter of a Chinese railroad worker. Several months later, the newlyweds moved to Shanghai, getting caught in the Boxer Rebellion. He continued his travels becoming a renowned explorer and adventurer.
>
> Eventually, Hargrove returned to Kansas City where one afternoon a mysterious, bespectacled gentleman appeared on his doorstep, informing him of his family's long-lost collection of art and antiquities dating back to the early 1800s. Soon thereafter, Gilbert met a tragic end when he was run over by a streetcar.

In this installation, we have re-created the den of the curious, nomadic Mr. Hargrove and showcased his own, as well as his ancestors' and descendants', eclectic collection.

But as I squinted down to the bottom of the panel I saw some small print in italics.

Gilbert G. Hargrove, his story, and his family are fictional and any resemblance to anyone living or dead is purely coincidental. The objects in this installation are taken from the collections of Scott Hefley and the Nelson-Atkins.

Needless to say, the exhibition was immense fun. The organizer(s) had been given an all-access pass to cut across the departmental boundaries of the great museum (boundaries that traditionally were inhospitable to cross), and they had been allowed to pick and chose the whimsical, the curious and the truly bizarre and, furthermore, to juxtapose them with utter disregard for chronology, geography, or any other known methodology for subdividing human knowledge. It's hard to know what the typical museum-goer might think upon wandering into a room essentially devoid of labels, explanations, or certainty of any kind. People don't normally go to museums in search of ambiguity; they expect to be told artist's names, dates, schools, isms, and other snippets of presumed truth. But welcome to the new museum, where the aim is often to generate questions rather than answers.

The Hargrove exhibition is accompanied by a small 44-page "family history", called *The Hargrove Family History*, written by "Tara Hargrove." (It's actually the work of Tara Varney and Bryan Colley, who are both Kansas City playwrights, among other creative endeavors.) The book is a lighthearted spoof on the stereotype of the eccentric collector, beginning with Perry Hargrove, born, rather suspiciously, on July 4, 1776, and whose collection included "such rarities as George Washington's wig, John Adams' spade, or his prized possession, the quill pen used by Thomas Jefferson to write the Declaration of Independence." Later generations of the family include Mortimer, a janitor at the Metropolitan Museum of Art, and his son Patrick, who forged Impressionist paintings, ending with his grandson, Roger, a Berkeley campus radical and drug addict who thought of museums as places "where art goes to die."

Increasingly, museums are rediscovering the usefulness of their quirky origins as cabinets of curiosities. In fact, another wonderfully-selected exhibition currently at the Nelson-Atkins is entitled "Cabinet of Curiosities: Photography & Specimens"). My guess is this trend got a bit of a push from the 1988 founding of the Museum of Jurassic Technology in Los Angeles, surely one of oddest collection of curiosities in the world. The MJT has a habit of taking all manner of ridiculous things very seriously and, in doing so, converting the overly-serious occasion of a museum visit into an outing that is comedic, theatrical, and provocative. When the work of artists and curators makes reference to the cabinet of curiosities it is usually calling several notions into play; it's a strategy that temporarily erases the distinctions between art and kitsch and utilitarian objects and that invokes a lost sense of awe and wonder as visitors encounter objects. Few gestures could be more antithetical to the longstanding image of museums than to throw out criteria such as authenticity and aesthetic judgment, but seems to be one way to encourage looking for its own sake.

The Hargrove Family History is cousin to books like William Boyd's hoax biography from 1998 of the non-existent abstract expressionist painter *Nat Tate, An American Artist: 1928-1960* and Leanne Shapton's 2009 book *Important Artifacts and Personal Property from the Collection of Lenore Doolan and Harold Morris, Including Books, Street Fashion, and Jewelry,* which purports to tell the story of a failed marriage through the items sent to auction after the divorce. A PDF version of *The Hargrove Family History* can be downloaded for free from the special website created for the exhibition. The fictional family biography contains a number of uncredited portrait photographs, most of which appear to have either been manipulated or posed, along with photographs of various objects attributed to the family collection.

This is actually the second time in recent months I've encountered an exhibition of genuine (or mostly genuine) objects built around the concept of fictitious collectors. Last fall, the London organization Artangel organized the exhibition "Nowhere Less Now," in which artist Lindsay Seers accumulated a fantastic number of objects into an old sea cadets home in London called the Tin Tabernacle. Every visitor to the exhibition was given a book by the same name, which is a marvelous, heavily illustrated fictional text about memory, codes, shipping, and much more, includes many photographs from private collections and public archives.

About the Authors

This book was created by Tara Varney and Bryan Colley to accompany *The Magnificent Collection of Gilbert G. Hargrove* exhibit at the Nelson-Atkins Museum of Art, which was on display from December 2012 to March 2013. The objects in this installation are taken from the collections of Scott Hefley and the Nelson-Atkins.

Tara Varney is an actor, playwright, director, and theatre educator from Kansas City, Missouri. She is a Dickens Caroler and teaches acting, theatre exploration, stage makeup, and digital storytelling for the Coterie Theatre, Young Audiences, CreativeWorks, and her own after-school program, Dramara-ma. She is the recipient of a 2012 ArtsKC Inspiration Grant for the play *Sexing Hitler*.

Bryan Colley is a playwright, screenwriter, and graphic designer who grew up in Sugar Creek, Missouri. He is a founding member of the Kansas City Screenwriters where he wrote the short films *Rhubarb Pie* and *Fringe Follies*. He is also a former president of the Just Off Broadway Theatre Association and curates *Offstage*, the *KC Stage* blog.

Together they have written and produced multiple "Best of Fringe" plays at the Kansas City Fringe Festival, including *Jesus Christ King of Comedy, Lingerie Shop, Khaaaaan! the Musical,* and *Hexing Hitler/Sexing Hitler.*

They would like to thank everyone at the Nelson-Atkins Museum that helped develop this project, including Rose May, Scott Heffley, Gaylord Torrence, Colin Mackenzie, Elisabeth Batchelor, Leesa Fanning, Amber Mills, Steve Waterman, and Judith Koke.

www.ingramcontent.com/pod-product-compliance
Lightning Source LLC
Chambersburg PA
CBHW021917170526
45157CB00005B/2088